JANE AUSTEN IN HER TIME

Jane Austen, by her sister, Cassandra Austen.
This is the only authentic portrait.

Jane Austen
IN HER TIME

W. A. CRAIK

NELSON

THOMAS NELSON AND SONS LTD
36 Park Street, London W1
P.O. Box 336, Apapa, Lagos
P.O. Box 25012, Nairobi
P.O. Box 21149, Dar es Salaam
P.O. Box 2187, Accra
77, Coffee Street, San Fernando, Trinidad

THOMAS NELSON (AUSTRALIA) LTD
597, Little Collins Street, Melbourne

THOMAS NELSON & SONS (SOUTH AFRICA) (PROPRIETARY) LTD
51, Commissioner Street, Johannesburg

THOMAS NELSON & SONS (CANADA) LTD
81, Curlew Drive, Don Mills, Ontario

17 135039 1

Phototypeset by Oliver Burridge Filmsetting Ltd, Crawley, Sussex
Made and printed in Great Britain by
William Clowes and Sons, Limited, London and Beccles
for Thomas Nelson and Sons Ltd, 36 Park Street, London W1

FOR LESLIE AND MARY DAW

CONTENTS

ILLUSTRATIONS

PREFACE

This book attempts to give the reader enough of the England of Jane Austen's time to enable him to read her novels with the understanding the author assumes he will possess. It cannot attempt to give a complete account of social conditions in England at the end of the eighteenth and beginning of the nineteenth centuries. The emphasis is mainly on the middle class, and mainly on the country, because Jane Austen's material lies here. The very rich, the permanent city-dwellers, and the urban poor are outside her scope as a novelist, and are not therefore so urgently needed by her reader. As much of the evidence as possible, and as many of the examples, have been taken from her own novels and her letters as are consonant with presenting a balanced view of her age. Where possible, other examples are from the writings of her contemporaries.

It is not essential to have read Jane Austen's novels or to know her life, to understand this book; although an acquaintance with one or two of them—which is what most readers already have—will be a help. The two appendixes provide a short biography of herself, and very brief synopses of what happens in the novels, to supply the very barest minimum of facts. I have not tried to capture the purpose or the flavour of the novels in these summaries; I hope rather that both may emerge from the numerous quotations in the body of the work.

Since this is not a series which offers detailed references for all the statements made, there is no bibliography appended. My more conspicuous debts are acknowledged in footnotes. I am generally indebted to G. M. Trevelyan's *Illustrated English Social History*, Longmans, 1952, and to Arthur Bryant's *The Age of Elegance*, Collins, 1942, for themselves and for the further authorities to which they led me in their turn.

In quoting from the novels and the letters, I have used the text of

R. W. Chapman's editions,[1] to which I am deeply indebted also for the material in their notes and invaluable appendixes. I have, however, identified quotations from the novels by chapter references in the numerical sequence used in the normal modern one-volume editions, rather than the three-volume numbering of Chapman and the first editions, as being easier for the ordinary reader to follow.

For the use of their facilities I am indebted to the staffs of the Aberdeen University Library, the British Museum, and the Victoria and Albert Museum. I gladly acknowledge also the help received in conversation with my friends and colleagues, particularly Professor Andrew Rutherford, Mr J. G. Roberts, and Mr Andrew F. Walls. The responsibility for any mistakes I have made is, however, entirely my own. My thanks are also due to Miss Gail Hawks for typing the manuscript, and to my husband for his invaluable and never-failing support.

Department of English,
King's College,
Old Aberdeen.

[1] *The Novels of Jane Austen*, ed. R. W. Chapman, five volumes, Oxford; third edition 1933, fifth impression 1953. *Jane Austen's Letters*, ed. R. W. Chapman, second edition, reprinted and corrected 1959.

CHAPTER ONE

Introduction

JANE Austen's England is the England of the years in which she wrote her novels; that is, from the 1790's to her death in 1816. It is the England of the Regency; of the Lake Poets Wordsworth and Coleridge; of Lord Byron; and of Cobbett's *Rural Rides*. But just as these all suggest a different view of life and what composes it, so the England, that which lies behind and is revealed in Jane Austen's novels, while frequently having much in common with Wordsworth's, or Byron's, or Cobbett's, or the Prince Regent's, does not necessarily include theirs, any more than theirs include each others'. To understand Jane Austen's times does not entail a comprehensive knowledge of the social history of her age as seen by a historian (valuable though such a knowledge is), since this would include much that is irrelevant to her world, and would unavoidably omit the minutiae of daily life, which are indispensable, yet which no general social history has space to include. The kind of accessory information that is so valuable when reading a novelist can be selected and assembled, not on historical principles, but only by understanding the novelist's own principles of selection from the life around him. Jane Austen, as is well known, is one whose principles entail great economy, and, hence, exclusion. As a consequence, she depends upon an understanding reader who, as well as being perceptive enough to appreciate her methods, is also as familiar and well informed as herself about the life and times of which she writes. She could legitimately and properly expect such a reader, in a society as coherent and stable as the England of her day still was. The appreciative and understanding reviews and notices of her novels as they appeared prove that she was a readily intelligible and popular writer. But times change, and with them manners, customs, and the whole paraphernalia of daily life, as well as attitudes and beliefs. While attitudes and beliefs are what a reader is first conscious of in the literature

Steventon Rectory, where Jane Austen lived until she was twenty-six.

of another age, as being different from his own, these, in a writer like Jane Austen, who deals with the least changing of them, cause relatively less difficulty than changes which the reader does not even notice. The general reader responds to the passion driving a man who rides from London to Somerset in twelve hours, who declares:

> 'the only ten minutes I have spent out of my chaise since that time, procured me a nuncheon at Marlborough.'

(*SS*, 43)

but the speech is even more powerful if he also knows, without having to puzzle, the route Willoughby must have taken, the nature of a chaise and the social position of a man who owns one, the amount of discomfort and speed entailed, and what a nuncheon is. These, as well as greater matters, are the kind of background Jane Austen needs.

Jane Austen's novels, like charity, begin at home. The centre of all her novels is a family or families, consisting usually of only two generations: parents, and children whose growing-up constitutes

The cottage at Chawton, near Alton, Hampshire, where Jane Austen lived until just before her death in 1817. It is now the Jane Austen Museum.

the novel's progress. The novels' happy conclusions all dismiss the heroines, not simply to ideal husbands, but to homes and families of their own. Though the stories may look like romances, in that they concern the adventures of their heroines which lead them to marriage, it is not these adventures for their own sake which Jane Austen cares about, but the way in which what happens prepares the heroine for the life that lies ahead of her, and enables her to choose the right life for herself. The right one for the guileless Catherine Morland, in *Northanger Abbey*, is as the wife of a cheerful and acute young clergyman; the right one for the lively Elizabeth Bennet, in *Pride and Prejudice*, is as the lady of a very rich country landowner; for Fanny Price, of *Mansfield Park*, one that keeps her still within the family and the estate that has made her what she is; for Emma, one that enables her to continue in what she already does so well, the duties of the lady of the manor; and for Anne Elliot, in *Persuasion*, one that will give her the full chance to live in the frank, loving, and useful society of the naval world.

Therefore what are most important to Jane Austen are personal

Godmersham Park, in Kent, the home of Jane Austen's brother, Edward Knight.

relationships between individuals; these are the materials with which she always works, and the terms in which she reveals her very serious preoccupations with personal morals and the individual's relation with his society. Since human nature in its essentials has not changed much over the centuries, and has not had time to change much in the 150-odd years between Jane Austen's time and our own, many of the most vital things in her novel are immediately intelligible. Her novels can amuse and enthral an intelligent child who knows nothing at all of the history and social conditions of England between 1811, when *Sense and Sensibility* was published, and 1817, when Jane Austen died. They can equally profit the foreigner who knows little of England but the language, who can recognise the universal application of many of her conclusions, and the universal truth of many of her characters and situations. It is tempting therefore to assume that Jane Austen is self-explanatory, and that she can be read by the light of nature—as indeed she can, in the sense that any great writer can stand on his own and speak direct to his hearers. But it is tempting to go further with Jane Austen, and to feel that, less than most writers, does she require her reader to know the world and the age which bred her, and a part of which she depicts. She

rarely alludes, like Scott, to events of her own time or the past, and she seems to offer no difficulties of language like those of earlier writers. But one does not read in her novels for long before discovering that things are not quite what they seem, that many details in Jane Austen's world differ slightly from those in one's own, and that such details have a significance that one cannot register if one does not really know the facts. One realises the difficulties even in the most popular and most readily appreciable *Pride and Prejudice*. The perceptive reader must soon ask himself what sort of a dinner is served by Mrs Bennet and what constitutes a 'course' when

> she did not think that anything less than two courses, could be good enough for a man, on whom she had such anxious designs, or satisfy the appetite and pride of one who had ten thousand a-year.
>
> (*PP*, 53)

He will also realise that, though ten thousand a-year is clearly a splendid income, he may not be sure *how* splendid, or how it compares with that of, for instance, a clergyman like Mr Collins. He finds that familiar landmarks in the day are not what he thought. He is not sure of the time at which this dinner is to be eaten, and discovers coffee and tea (which now suggest morning and afternoon) are apparently drunk some time during the evening. Such disturbances of what it seems safe to assume are, though slight, continuous. Lady Catherine de Bourgh remarks:

> 'This must be a most inconvenient sitting room for the evening, in summer; the windows are full west.'
> Mrs Bennett assured her that they never sat there after dinner.
>
> (*PP*, 56)

While this reveals something about the time of dinner, it is a surprise to learn that a sunny room is not considered an advantage. This surprise reinforces an earlier one, when the jealous Miss Bingley commented that Elizabeth has 'grown so brown and coarse', and Mr Darcy

> contented himself with replying, that he perceived no other altera-tion than her being rather tanned—no miraculous consequence of travelling in the summer.
>
> (*PP*, 45)

Clearly a sun-tan is not a thing to strive after, and no asset even in the eyes of a lover. The sense of being imperfectly informed by the novelist of what is plainly necessary information may be felt on more serious matters, as when Jane Austen, concluding her story, remarks of Lydia and her profligate husband Wickham:

> Their manner of living, even when the restoration of peace dismissed them to a home, was unsettled in the extreme.
>
> (*PP*, 61)

War has never been mentioned hitherto, and it is a sophisticated and acute reader indeed who has postulated it from the presence of a militia regiment in the early part of the novel—and, if it comes to that, what is the difference between the militia and the regular army?

Such questions as these soon begin to intrude upon any keen reader of Jane Austen's works. Many of them are questions to which the novels themselves will, if pressed, supply the answer. Many more can be answered by recourse to books of reference, or social histories. Some few, very minor, are very difficult to answer at all (like the constitution and significance of the 'white soup' that Mr Bingley provides at the ball he gives at Netherfield). But there is a fourth class of question and answer which is more difficult for the casual reader either to ask or answer, and that is the one that the text never itself suggests, but a knowledge of which inevitably affects how the reader responds. The simplest example at this point is money, which looms so large in all Jane Austen's writing that she has sometimes been thought mercenary. But a man in 1800 was alone in the world from manhood to the grave. He could expect no help in adversity from any but himself, his family, or 'charity'. He must work or starve. Illness must be paid for when there is no state scheme. If he married, he must support all his (probably many) children, through illnesses made more dangerous by the lack of medical skill and knowledge. He must work until the day he died, unless he could save enough to live on in retirement. For women things are worse, as few professions are open to them, and none of them agreeable; marriage, as one character bluntly says

> was the only honourable provision for well-educated young woman of small fortune, and however uncertain of giving happiness, must be their pleasantest preservative from want.
>
> (*PP*, 22)

As David Cecil so neatly put it: 'It is wrong to marry for money, but silly to marry without it.' Jane Austen assumes that her readers know the answers to all these questions as well as she does herself. She assumes that they already know all the trivial and everyday details of the life of her time, and the life that surrounds and awaits her heroines. She can rightly assume that most details of life in a country rectory, as led by the heroines Catherine Morland, Elinor Dashwood, and Fanny Price, or of the life awaiting the wife of a naval officer, like Anne Elliot, or of a landowner, like Elizabeth Bennet or Emma, will be perfectly familiar and be supplied by the reader for himself. Within the action of the novel itself, she mentions the impedimenta of everyday living—food, clothes, furniture, servants, people's occupations—only where the actual conduct of her story demands. She never indulges in detailed descriptions for the sake of local colour, or for its own sake; and she again depends on the reader to do a good deal of the work for himself.

She is equally reticent over greater matters. Her novels touch upon and suggest many things outside the 'three or four families in a Country Village' which she commended to her niece as 'the very

thing to work on'[1] in a novel. Soldier and sailor characters imply a
knowledge of the army and navy of her time, which she is known
to have had, especially as two of her brothers became admirals.
She frequently moves the action of her novels to parts of the
country other than her native Hampshire and the southern
counties, to Derbyshire in *Pride and Prejudice*, or Northamptonshire
in *Mansfield Park*; and moves from the country to the city, notably
to London, Bath, and Portsmouth. Here again she mentions only
what immediately concerns her, while much that she and her
readers both knew well is left out.

Even more fundamental matters, such as the whole structure of
society from the highest to the lowest, the many revolutionary
developments during her lifetime in political thinking, in
philosophy, in literature and the other arts, she barely hints at. A
twentieth-century reader of Jane Austen may deduce from what
she writes that the Romantic revival in literature is well underway,
but would probably not be able to postulate all that is implied by
the word 'regency', or even the existence of the Prince Regent, to
whom, at his own request, she dedicated *Emma*. He might deduce
the interest in the Gothic in literature (from the burlesque in
Northanger Abbey) but not the Gothic revival beginning in architecture. The whole world of national politics, of the industrial
revolution, of Europe inflamed with revolutions and struggles for
power, the world containing Cobbett, Nelson, the Duke of
Wellington, Napoleon, Blücher, and Prince Metternich is,
apparently, ignored.

In such international matters as in domestic ones, Jane Austen
assumes a great deal of common knowledge in her reader. The
reader cannot think, because Jane Austen apparently calls upon
so small a part of the life of her time, that the rest of it does not
matter to her. Her letters prove that she gave a great deal of time
and thought to matters never emphasised in her novels, and a
familiarity with such matters and others besides is invaluable, not
only to understanding more fully the significance of her novels,
both in their entirety and in small details, but also to appreciating
the greatness of her achievement and the perfection of her art.

Unfortunately the lapse of over 150 years since her death has
gradually deprived her readers of much common information

[1] Letter to Anna Austen, 9 September 1814.

The house in College Street, Winchester, where Jane Austen died on
18 July 1817.

upon which Jane Austen thought, very properly, that she could
depend. It is the purpose of this book to supply some of the most
essential of this information, and so to put the twentieth-century

reader somewhere near the reader for whom Jane Austen wrote her novels. Parodying Scott, she once said

> I do not write for such dull elves
> As have not a great deal of ingenuity themselves.

To know the world of which and for which she is writing is to give oneself the constant pleasure of proving one's ingenuity by recognising Jane Austen's.

The course of this book is to begin with the central and vital, which is probably also the most familiar, which depends a great deal on expanding, elaborating, and explaining topics that Jane Austen herself mentions; and to move thence to the more general topics, which are more often implicit than explicit in what she writes. This means beginning with the often apparently trivial— as she herself is sometimes accused of being trivial—with home life, and then moving from domestic matters as experienced by the people in what Scott calls the 'middling class of society, or slightly lower' in the country, to the ways they were brought up, educated, and behaved, the ways in which they earned their livings and spent their lives, the ideas, pleasures and culture available to them, country life and society in general, the town and the city, and all the hazards and opportunities of life at the end of the eighteenth and beginning of the nineteenth centuries.

CHAPTER TWO

The Trivial Round

LIFE under the Regency at the beginning of the nineteenth century was not static, any more than it ever was, or is now. Fashions in living change with habits of thought, and the results in life are often a mixture of the old and the new. A passage in which Jane Austen shows that she is herself well aware of the fact occurs in her last, and perhaps her most explicit, novel, *Persuasion*, when the heroine, Anne Elliot, newly arrived on a visit to her sister, goes to pay a formal call upon that sister's parents-in-law:

> To the Great House accordingly they went, to sit the full half hour in the old-fashioned square parlour, with a small carpet and shining floor, to which the present daughters of the house were gradually giving the proper air of confusion by a grand piano forte and a harp, flower-stands and little tables placed in every direction. Oh! could the originals of the portraits against the wainscot, could the gentlemen in brown velvet and the ladies in blue satin have seen what was going on, have been conscious of such an overthrow of all order and neatness! The portraits themselves seemed to be staring in astonishment.
>
> The Musgroves, like their houses, were in a state of alteration, perhaps of improvement. The father and mother were in the old English style, and the young people in the new. Mr and Mrs Musgrove were a very good sort of people; friendly and hospitable, not much educated, and not at all elegant. Their children had more modern minds and manners.

(P, 5)

Although within 'the middling classes of society', in which Jane Austen lived and about which she writes, ways of life vary, and although it would be idle to construct the representative 'day in the life', so beloved of elementary school-books, yet daily life is plainly the first thing to consider, and one must venture to make a number of fairly safe generalisations. One thing certain, both from

SENSE

AND

SENSIBILITY:

A NOVEL.

IN THREE VOLUMES.

BY A LADY.

VOL. I.

London:

PRINTED FOR THE AUTHOR,

By *C. Roworth, Bell-yard, Temple-bar,*

AND PUBLISHED BY T. EGERTON, WHITEHALL.

1811.

The title page of the first edition of *Sense and Sensibility*, 1811.

Jane Austen's novels and from other contemporary sources, is that ways of living did not vary very violently, within quite a wide band of society and different degrees of wealth. From *Emma* alone, one can see that daily life in the home, as lived by the aged widow of a vicar and her daughter in a few rooms on the main street of a Surrey village—exemplified by the minor characters Mrs Bates and Miss Bates of Highbury—is not very different, in its routine and conduct, from that lived by a young woman who, though not married, is mistress of the most prosperous house in the neighbourhood—the position held by the heroine Emma Woodhouse herself at Hartfield. Miss Bates can be visited by Emma and her father, or the other landowner, Mr Knightley, and can return their social calls, without any sense that either is moving into another class. Each finds the same kind of behaviour, and the same ways of doing things, even though, as Mr Knightley says, Miss Bates 'is poor; she has sunk from the comforts she was born to; and if she live to old age, must probably sink more' (*E*, 44). This is not to deny that class distinctions exist in Jane Austen's novels and in the society on which she draws; but they do not affect the conduct of daily life as much as one might assume, nor are they even easy to chart, when, as turns out to be the case in *Sense and Sensibility* for instance, the daughters of a very minor attorney in Bristol are able to adapt themselves to the habits (if not the manners) both of the household and easy-going ways of one country landowner, and to the polished social round as lived in the London house of another one.

The conduct of the ordinary affairs of the ordinary day was arranged rather differently from any modern one, in ways that can prove puzzling when one is not aware of the differences. When the day begins is somewhat a matter of personal choice, since breakfast is both a later and a more formal affair than its modern equivalent—and continued to be so even in the century after Jane Austen writes: years after Jane Austen, the famous Victorian John Ruskin does two hours' work before breakfasting. *Mansfield Park* gives probably more details of the life of the large but not aristocratic country house than any other of Jane Austen's novels; in it we find that Henry Crawford, himself a landowner, but staying as a guest at the vicarage, is invited to breakfast before journeying down to London with William, the nephew of the house, whom he has invited to travel with him in his carriage. The breakfast provided, probably at the usual hour of ten o'clock in the morning, is a fairly substantial affair, as is suggested by 'the remaining cold pork bones and mustard in William's plate' and 'the broken egg-shells in Mr Crawford's' over which the heroine, Fanny, is 'left to cry in peace' (*MP*, 29). When the reader knows that this sort of breakfast, at this sort of time, is the norm, the determination of that most romantic and enthusiastic heroine Marianne Dashwood, in *Sense and Sensibility*, 'never to be later in rising than six, and from that time till dinner . . . divide every moment between music and reading' (*SS*, 45) is seen in all its formidable resolution.

After breakfast the day continues without formal interruption until dinner, whose hour varies according to the inclination, age, and pretensions to fashion of the household, being generally (then as now) later in London than elsewhere. Four o'clock is an early hour, suiting the old-fashioned and fairly countrified habits of Emma's father Mr Woodhouse; the pretentious but not up-to-date or fashionable General Tilney in *Northanger Abbey* dines exactly at five; the stylish Bingleys, bringing their London ways into Hertfordshire in *Pride and Prejudice*, dine as late as half-past six. The whole period between breakfast and dinner is called 'morning' in Jane Austen's day, and is the time for all the day's business. An imaginative and extremely efficient man of business of the period, Thomas Love Peacock, now remembered as a witty novelist rather than as Chief Examiner with the East India Company, versified his working day with a self-mockery that must not be taken seriously:

> From ten to eleven, ate a breakfast for seven;
> From eleven to noon, to begin was too soon;
> From twelve to one, asked 'What's to be done?'
> From one to two found nothing to do;
> From two to three began to foresee
> That from three to four would be a damned bore.

After four he went home for dinner.

Peacock's working day is also the period during which formal calls are paid, so that the formal little visits of fifteen minutes' duration, which figure in the novels, in Jane Austen's own letters, and in the life of middle-class women throughout the nineteenth century, are termed 'morning' calls, even though they were made throughout what is now called the afternoon—a term Jane Austen only rarely uses. It would be quite wrong to suppose that Jane Austen's women have nothing else, or better, to do than pay calls —and their occupations and duties will be dealt with in due course; nevertheless the paying of calls looms large, for two reasons: first that they are a very necessary means of keeping in touch with the life and social concerns of a neighbourhood, allowing varying degrees of acquaintance where close friendship is not desired; and second, that they often serve Jane Austen's artistic purposes as a novelist, being the occasions on which social situations develop, information is exchanged, or relationships between characters revealed. In *Pride and Prejudice*, Jane Bennet, who has been sought in friendship by Miss Bingley and her sister Mrs Hurst, who have had her to stay with them for whole-day visits, realises, when she gets to London, that they want no more to do with her, when they call on her for no more than the cool and formal fifteen minutes, despite their former intimacy. Emma Woodhouse uses the same convention to show the farming family, the Martins, whom she wishes to separate from her newly acquired friend Harriet, that she thinks them not good enough for her:

> they were just growing again like themselves, (Harriet, as Emma must suspect, as ready as the best of them to be cordial and happy), when the carriage re-appeared, and all was over. The style of the visit, and the shortness of it, were then felt to be decisive. Fourteen minutes to be given to those with whom she had thankfully passed six weeks not six months ago!
>
> (*E*, 23)

An entertaining account of these formal fifteen-minute calls, recollected by one to whom they are an old-fashioned custom, is Mrs Gaskell's in *Cranford*:

> 'I dare say your mamma has told you, my dear, never to let more than three days elapse between receiving a call and returning it; and also, that you are never to stay longer than a quarter of an hour.'
>
> 'But am I to look at my watch? How am I to find out when a quarter of an hour has passed?'

'You must keep thinking about the time, my dear, and not allow
yourself to forget it in conversation.'

As everybody had this rule in their minds, whether they received
or paid a call, of course no absorbing subject was ever spoken about.

(*Cranford*, Ch. 1)

The difficulties Jane Austen recognises are not of remembering
the time but of making conversation. A longer visit reveals a closer
degree of acquaintance, as when Anne Elliot, in the passage
already quoted, goes to Uppercross 'to sit the full half hour' (*P*, 5)
with her sister's parents-in-law; or it may also indicate the desire
for greater friendship: Mr Darcy, demonstrating his change of
manners and heart to Elizabeth in *Pride and Prejudice*, calls with
his sister 'on the very morning after their own arrival'—a compliment in itself—and 'stayed with them above half an hour' (*PP*, 44)
—suggesting another.

A mid-day meal intervenes very informally during the morning;
so informally as to have apparently neither an official time nor
name, and consisting of food easily eaten without a properly laid
table—cold meat, sandwiches, cake, and fruit. Anne Elliot,
arriving at Uppercross, finds her sister Mary lying on the sofa
imagining she is ill, but soon 'forgetting to think of it, she was at the
other end of the room, beautifying a nosegay; then she ate her
cold meat; and then she was well enough to propose a little walk'
(*P*, 5), and the activities of the morning continue. It is a meal for
which no invitations are given, although visitors who happen to be
present may stay for it, as Fanny Price and Edmund Bertram,
calling at the parsonage from Mansfield Park, listen to Mary
Crawford playing the harp, and share in the contents of 'the
sandwich tray' (*MP*, 7). Jane Austen never calls this meal by the
word 'luncheon', which a modern reader feels inclined to bestow
on it, although the word existed and was used by her outside the
novels. Luncheon generally means a small snack taken between
meals, and is at this period equivalent to the 'nuncheon' of cold
meat and porter that is all Willoughby allows himself, in *Sense and
Sensibility*, on his desperate ride from London to Somerset when he
believes that Marianne is dying.

The formal meal of the day is dinner, at whatever time it is
taken. It is perhaps the most important regular social occasion in
the novels, as the time at which people reassemble from their

various individual pursuits. It is taken seriously, not only by serious eaters, like the *bon vivant* clergyman Dr Grant, of *Mansfield Park*, or by sticklers for status like Mrs Norris, warning her niece Fanny 'not to be taking place of' Miss Crawford when invited to dine with the Doctor, but also by serious house-keepers like Mrs Bennet of *Pride and Prejudice*, who 'did not think anything less than two courses could . . . satisfy the appetite and pride of one who had ten thousand a-year' (*PP*, 53).

Even so, the rules are not as strict as later, in the Victorian period. It clearly does not matter, as it would have done to a Victorian hostess, and possibly even to a modern one, whether the numbers of men and women are equal; they frequently are not, and when Mr John Knightley, arriving unexpectedly, makes nine at his sister-in-law Emma's party, she does not consider finding another lady to even up the number. The dinner itself was differently constituted from a modern one. The 'course' (of which Mrs Bennet feels compelled to offer two) was a complete laying of the table, almost a dinner in itself, with a main dish, and all the subsidiary dishes that accompanied it, all of which were placed at the appropriate point on the table. This quite extensive operation, with all guests present, would, even when performed by adept servants, convincingly explain the break in conversation when Emma dines at the Coles':

> The conversation was here interrupted. They were called on to share in the awkwardness of a rather long interval between courses, and obliged to be as formal and orderly as the others. But when the table was again safely covered, when every corner dish was again exactly right,
>
> (*E*, 26)

then the talk may resume.

The quantity and type of food varies according to income and taste. Jane Austen herself in her letters gives details of modest meals, eaten by their own small family: on one occasion, when her elder sister is away, and she is in charge of the housekeeping,

> We sat down to dinner a little after five, and had some beef-steaks and a boiled fowl, but no oyster sauce.

on another,

> I have had some ragout veal, and I mean to have some haricot

mutton tomorrow . . . I am very fond of experiments in housekeeping such as having an oxcheek now and then; I shall have one next week, and I mean to have some little dumplings put into it.

on a third, when a visitor called unexpectedly and 'partook of our elegant entertainment',

I was not ashamed of asking him to sit down at table, for we had some pease-soup, a spare-rib, and a pudding.[1]

She also alludes to an occasion on which her sister Cassandra was at supper with Prince William of Gloucester, apropos of which R. W. Chapman, in his edition of Jane Austen's letters, gives the menu for a dinner provided for the prince by the Dean of Canterbury.

> *Salmon Trout*
> *Soles*
> *Fricando of Veal. Rais'd Giblet Pie*
> *Vegetable Pudding*
> *Chickens. Ham*
> *Muffin Pudding*
> *Curry of Rabbits. Preserve of Olives*
> *Soup. Haunch of Venison*
> *Open Tart Syllabub. Rais'd Jelly*
> *Three Sweetbreads, larded*
> *Maccaroni. Buttered Lobster*
> *Peas*
> *Potatoes*
> *Baskets of Pastry. Custards*
> *Goose*

When dinner is over, the ladies retire to the drawing-room for coffee, leaving the men to take wine in the dining room, from which they join the ladies individually, as and when they choose, again unlike the formal mass re-entry after a Victorian dinner. At one party we hear that 'they were very soon joined by some of the

---

[1] Letters to Cassandra Austen, Wednesday 24 October, Saturday 17 November, and Saturday 1 December 1798.

gentlemen; and the very first of the early was Frank Churchill'
(*E*, 26), and at another:

> Mr Woodhouse very soon followed them into the drawing-room.
> To be sitting long after dinner was a confinement he could not
> endure. Neither wine nor conversation was anything to him; and
> gladly did he move to those with whom he was always comfortable.
>
> (*E*, 14)

The last official function of the day is tea, with which goes some
sort of light refreshment, some hours after dinner if that has been
an early one, and at the end of the stay of any guests there may
have been. The intervening interval is filled with some sort of
recreation. At Emma's Hartfield, where they keep early hours—
and old-fashioned ones—to please Mr Woodhouse, there can be
walks with friends; but the more usual scheme involves conversation, music, and cards. Visitors may come for the evening, without
the dinner, as Lady Catherine de Bourgh in *Pride and Prejudice*
invites Elizabeth Bennet and the Collinses, when she already has
her nephews staying with her. Tea, as now, is an occasion rather
than a beverage, a light supper which, like the mid-day cold meat,
is not eaten at a table, or formally set out.

Jane Austen does occasionally mention supper. Elizabeth
Bennet's vulgar aunt Mrs Phillips invites her nieces and some
officers to a card party with 'a little bit of hot supper afterwards'
(*PP*, 15); while Emma's father Mr Woodhouse 'loved to have the
cloth laid, because it had been the fashion of his youth' (*E*, 3). He
himself wants only gruel, and recommends to his guests soft-boiled
eggs, apple tart, and custard, while they are 'comfortably clearing
the nicer things'; unhappily Jane Austen does not say what these
were, although on another occasion she mentions 'a delicate
fricassee of sweetbread and some asparagus' which, sadly,
Mrs Bates is not allowed to eat, because 'good Mr Woodhouse, not
thinking the asparagus quite boiled enough, sent it all out again'
(*E*, 38) leaving her only baked apples and biscuits. Supper is old-
fashioned, and thereby unfashionable, as are a number of other
old-fashioned things at this period; Mrs Phillips, providing it,
provides additional proof of her inelegance.

A certain amount of incidental and social eating takes place
also as an accessory to morning calls; refreshments are offered to
Elizabeth Bennet and her aunt and uncle at Pemberley: 'cold

meat, cake, and a variety of all the finest fruits in season ... beautiful pyramids of grapes, nectarines, and peaches' (*PP*, 45) and even the humble Miss Bates offers baked apples to Emma and Harriet.

Into this general pattern for the day fit 'all the numberless goings-on of life': the serious ones, like the upbringing of children, the education and occupations of young people before marriage, the household responsibilities of wives, the professions and occupations of men (which will occupy a separate chapter); the many forms which amusement can take: visiting, games, dancing, sports; and the numerous small obligations that are neither wholly duties, nor wholly amusements, such as newspapers, and letter-writing.

Visits play a considerable part in the novels, but an even more considerable one in Jane Austen's life, as her letters prove. Since travel took longer, and was expensive, whether private or public, visits of anything beyond the social call or the dinner engagement tend to be, by modern standards, very long indeed, running as often into months as into weeks. Jane Austen herself spent months with her brother, Edward, in Kent, and weeks with another brother, Henry, in London. In the novels, Elizabeth Bennet, on her memorable visit to Hunsford and Rosings, stays six weeks; and when her scapegrace sister Lydia and Lydia's scapegrace husband Wickham, newly and at last married, visit Longbourn before going to Newcastle, they make a very short stay, of only ten days. We therefore should have some real sympathy for Mr Woodhouse saying 'in a very depressed tone' that his daughter is coming 'for only one week. There will not be time for anything' (*E*, 9). When visiting, guests were absorbed into the common life of the place where they stayed, and continued with their ordinary pursuits, as did their hosts, with very little that was extraordinary in the way of entertainment. The normal routine of the day prevails. The characters in the novels who provide treats for their guests are the oddities, not altogether to be approved: Mrs Bennet, in *Pride and Prejudice*, 'had so carefully provided for the entertainment of her brother and sister, that they did not once sit down to a family dinner'; Elizabeth wryly comments, 'You know my mother's ideas as to the necessity of constant company for her friends' (*PP*, 25).

Holidays must likewise be longer. Elizabeth is disappointed of her tour to the Lakes with this same aunt and uncle, because a month is not considered long enough to go as far from London as Westmorland and Cumberland, so she has to be content with Derbyshire. In *Mansfield Park*, Fanny's visit to her parents at Portsmouth is offered as a holiday by her uncle, when she has refused to marry Henry Crawford, and intended to last two months, even though it turns out a much longer plunge into a life so uncongenial that

> though Sir Thomas, had he known all, might have thought his niece in the most promising way of being starved, both in mind and body, into a much juster value for Mr Crawford's good company and good fortune, he would probably have feared to push his experiment farther, lest she might die under the cure.
>
> (*MP*, 42)

But the most important and the commonest social meeting is the dinner engagement, or the evening visit following it, to which most forms of amusement lend themselves, whether the visit is to a private house, or to a place of public entertainment, such as the Crown Inn at Highbury, where Emma and her neighbours have their Ball, or the local Assembly Rooms, such as those at Basingstoke visited by Jane Austen herself when, as a young woman, she lived at nearby Steventon. It is incidentally interesting to realise that such engagements were timed to fall on or near the full moon, with the light nights it brings—an important consideration in an age without even gas for lighting. Jane Austen mentions this point only once, when Sir John Dashwood, in *Sense and Sensibility*, trying to collect an impromptu party, 'had been to several families that morning in the hopes of procuring some addition to their number, but it was moonlight and every body was full of engagements' (*SS*, 7).

At such meetings as this one, games formed a large part of the entertainment. Along with music, conversation, and dancing, cards constitute the staple. Every dance, even, had its card room, for chaperones and older members of the party, such as Mr Allen

Card-playing at the Upper Rooms, Bath.

in *Northanger Abbey*, who, having delivered his wife and the heroine to the Upper Rooms at Bath, 'repaired directly to the card-room, and left them to enjoy a mob by themselves' (*NA*, 2). Many different games are played, from the still familiar whist and cribbage, played at Mansfield, to other now obsolete ones, like the piquet and loo played by the Bingleys at Netherfield. Others are mentioned calling for less skill than these, such as cassino, commerce, lottery tickets, quadrille, speculation, and vingt-et-un. All these, like most card games, are gambling games, and while those played in the family circle may not be played as such, it is certain that many of them are. In *Pride and Prejudice*, when Elizabeth Bennet is at Netherfield

> On entering the drawing-room she found the whole party at loo, and was immediately invited to join them; but suspecting them to be playing high, she declined it.
> (*PP*, 8)

Later on Mr Collins makes himself ridiculous when, having lost at Mrs Phillips's 'nice comfortable noisy game of lottery tickets' (*PP*, 15), he congratulates himself that he is 'happily not in such circumstances as to make five shillings any object' (*PP*, 16). Doubtless this is playing low. But this is the age of wagers, when fortunes changed hands in reckless bets on prize-fights and horses, and over cards at clubs, by comparison with which such small sums as Jane Austen deals in are innocent in intention, and harmless in effect.

Besides cards, people amuse themselves with what are now children's games: with the well-known 'consequences', with making anagrams, and with backgammon, a board game somewhat like draughts, but involving the use of dice.

The other great indoor evening amusement is dancing, which formed a large part of the social intercourse of a country neighbourhood, and of the seaside towns and spas, which Jane Austen chooses as her settings. Dances are of course quite formal at public places like the Upper Rooms at Bath, or the Assembly Rooms at market and assize towns such as Northampton, to which William wished he could take Fanny Price from Mansfield, or such as Basingstoke, to which Jane Austen went herself. Private dances are variously less formal, right down to the impromptu family affair for which Anne Elliot plays country dances for the Musgroves at Uppercross. But conventions must be observed even at the least formal, as the behaviour of Willoughby and the unconventional Marianne reveals, in *Sense and Sensibility*:

> If dancing formed the amusement of the night, they were partners for half the time; and when obliged to separate for a couple of dances, were careful to stand together and never spoke a word to anybody else. Such conduct of course made them both exceedingly

Plate from a dancing manual, showing different dance steps.

laughed at; but ridicule could not shame, and seemed hardly to provoke them.

(SS, 10)

The formal dances, like those at Bath, are regulated by a Master of Ceremonies, one of whose good offices is to provide people with properly introduced partners, as Henry Tilney, in *Northanger Abbey*, is introduced to Catherine. Girls are chaperoned by older, or married, women; hence the joke for Lydia, the youngest of the Bennet girls in *Pride and Prejudice*: 'Lord! how I should like to be married before any of you; and then I would chaperon you about to all the balls' (*PP*, 39).

Precedence, observed meticulously here as in so many other things, determines that the most important lady shall open the ball. This, to Fanny's surprise, is Fanny herself, at what is virtually her coming-out ball at Mansfield, and, to Emma's chagrin, is the new bride Mrs Elton, at the ball at the Crown. Thereafter the order in which sets are made up is free. The most popular dances are country-dances (from the French *contre-danse*, because one stands opposite other dancers) performed in sets by groups of couples, like Scottish dances and the still-found Sir Roger de Coverley. Hence the amount of time for conversation, while the participants are waiting their turn to reach the busiest points as top or bottom couple. These country dances form the greater proportion, although a ball usually opens with the old-fashioned minuet, and although the waltz was beginning to sweep its way in from the Continent. But the waltz was thought scandalous and improper even in the aristocratic circles frequented by Lord Byron (he wrote a poem deploring it) and therefore would not be seen in the more decorous ones of which Jane Austen writes.

Refreshments are an important part of a ball, and are substantial —at private balls at least. Lady Lucas in *Pride and Prejudice*, wearied by Mrs Bennet's 'repetition of delights [in getting a daughter married] which she saw no likelihood of sharing, was left to the comforts of cold ham and chicken' (*PP*, 18) at a supper to which the whole party sits down at the same time. There is no order of precedence in the seating, or Mrs Bennet would not be so unfortunately close to Mr Darcy. A ball must have proper food: 'A private dance, without sitting down to supper, was pronounced an infamous fraud upon the rights of men and women' (*E*, 29), and when this one in *Emma* actually takes place, it even begins with the serving of tea and coffee.

While balls at places like Bath might be as large as modern dances, generally even formal ones were very much smaller. Jane Austen's letters mention, without any surprise, balls at Basingstoke Assembly Rooms of only seventeen couples, with another twenty-odd people not dancing.[1] Private balls vary: eighteen couple of dancers are mentioned in *Sense and Sensibility* (35); in *Emma*, though five couple is rejected—'it will not do to *invite* five couple. It can be allowable only as the thought of a moment' (*E*, 29)—ten couple evidently constitute a proper dance in a private house. More people would be present, of course, though not dancing. A private, unpremeditated dance needs only a piano for music, and even a public one would have only a few instruments. The presence of a violin player in the servants' hall is enough for a dance (of five couple) even at the rather stately Mansfield Park (*MS*, 12).

During the earlier hours of the day when, apart from serious duties, for women 'its solace is visiting and news', men turn to sport. Fox-hunting is a popular and comparatively new sport, which in the mid-eighteenth century replaced hare-coursing. Jane Austen mentions it as a happiness of his holiday at Mansfield for the young midshipman William Price, and allows Willoughby's prowess in it in *Sense and Sensibility* to prove no evidence of virtue. The recent and still continuing enclosures of the old open fields, with hedges and ditches, which went on alongside the sport's popularity, made it both exciting and hazardous, and such as to merit Fanny's anxiety about William's safety. Hunting is expensive, for the enthusiast must buy and keep the horses, so keeping hunters is a sign that Willoughby is living beyond his means; on the other hand, Mansfield wealth is manifest when Edmund, the younger son, possesses hunters as well as a road horse; Mrs Norris is clearly therefore cheese-paring when thinking that it would be too extravagant to get a horse for Fanny.

Shooting is only for the privileged. Laws against poaching were stringent and punishments vicious, from the immediate hazards of man-trap and spring-gun to the prospect of seven years' transportation if caught. Partridge and pheasant are the only game

---

[1] Letter to Cassandra Austen, Saturday 1 November 1800.

Fox-hunting, which was still a comparatively new sport.

birds relevant to Jane Austen, since she does not write of grouse country. Partridges were stalked through the long corn-stubble, and pheasants flushed by spaniels out of hedges and woods. Greater skill was required then than now, with the more clumsy muzzle-loading flint and steel guns—rendering even more silly Mrs Bennet's invitation to Mr Bingley to come to them when he had killed all his own birds.

Jane Austen ignores other masculine amusements, even such rural ones as cricket, which, though a rustic game, was also one in which the gentry could join. Nor does she have anything to say about boxing, or rather, prize-fighting, whose enormous popularity could not be suspected from her work. To fill in such gaps, which Jane Austen and her readers knew well, one must go to other writers, and discover them from the ebullient enthusiasms of, for instance, the essayist William Hazlitt. To know about Tom Cribb, Sayers, and other famous 'pugs' and members of 'the fancy' is not essential in reading Jane Austen, but it is useful, and points again to the discretion with which she left things out. Her men are indicated by the bare minimum necessary to realise them, and one could never deduce, from Jane Austen, that this is the age when

A prize fight between the two 'pugs', Gully and Gregson.

20,000 people might foregather for a prize-fight, which, though it might seem noble to Hazlitt or to Lord Althorp (who called it 'worthy of Homer') was yet, when undertaken by men using their bare fists, fighting foot to foot without feinting or dodging, with the fight ending only when one of the two was slogged into submission, a brutal business, and at last, because of the size and extent of the bets laid, became also a dishonest one, with fights 'fixed' and victories sold.

Of indoor amusements for men billiards is the chief, at which Mr Palmer of *Sense and Sensibility* wastes his time. Always a popular game, it had a revival at the turn of the century. An advertisement in the *Morning Post* of 28 September 1809 declares:

> Billiards are becoming very fashionable: it is an amusement of a gentlemanly cast—giving at once activity to the limbs, and grace to the person.

The site of the disastrous Mansfield theatricals is the billiard-room, demonstrating that billiards has an established place in a gentleman's residence.

Newspapers, then as now, occupied a middle place between mere amusement and serious duty. They had been firmly established as a part of daily life since the middle of the eighteenth century. Circulation figures are not large: while 2,000 is high, and *The Times* in 1795 reached 4,800, the *Morning Post's* only 350. There were also provincial papers of repute such as the *Northamptonshire Mercury*, which Jane Austen could have used, had she wished, as that taken by the household of Mansfield Park.

A newspaper consisted of four folio pages of four columns, one or more of them taken up with advertisements for books, concerts, theatres, dress-makers and people wanting various kinds of domestic employment. The main body of the paper reported parliamentary debates, and foreign affairs. The rest was Gazette announcements, letters, gossip, articles and poems. Such a paper Mr Palmer is reading in *Sense and Sensibility* when, asked whether there is any news in it ' "No, none at all", he replied, and read on' (*SS*, 19).

News did not get 'cold' so quickly then as now, and newspapers reached many more people than the circulation figures suggest, being handed on and passed down the scale of wealth and rank from the original purchasers. The paper Mr Palmer reads is one that has been pressed upon Mrs Dashwood and her daughters by their good-natured landlord, Mr Palmer's brother-in-law, Sir John Middleton.

Private news is as vital as public news, and the transmission of it, by letters, took up a considerable part of many women's day. All the novels contain at least one very important letter. It is important therefore to be aware of the etiquette governing their writing and receiving, and of their actual appearance. When families and friends are at inconvenient distances, and visits, though long, are few, the letter is a necessary means of communication. Correspondence on matters other than business being women's concern, letter-writing should be one of a young lady's accomplishments— an accomplishment which Lady Bertram has, in her way, practised and perfected:

The Times of 7 November 1805, reporting the death of Nelson at Trafalgar.

The Times.

NUMBER 6572. LONDON, THURSDAY, NOVEMBER 7, 1805. PRICE SIXPENCE.

EUROPEAN MUSEUM.

GERRARD DOW's celebrated PICTURE of the DOUBLE SURPRISE, is arrived at the above National Gallery. The Nobility and Gentry, who wish to become subscribers for the ensuing season, are requested to be early in their application, as the Books will soon be closed.

J. WILSON, Manager.

Hours from 12 to 4. Admittance 1s.

WEST INDIA DOCK COMPANY.

THE COURT of DIRECTORS of the WEST INDIA DOCK COMPANY do hereby give notice, that a CALL of 25l. per Cent. is required to be paid into the funds of Messrs. Smith, Payne and Smiths, Mansion-house-street, on or before Thursday, the 5th day of December next, being the third Instalment on the last West India Dock additional Subscription of 100,000l.

By Order of the Court of Directors.

THOS. MARSHAM, Sec.

West India Dock House, 5th Nov. 1805.

LORD MAYOR's DAY.—FIVE GUINEAS will be given to any person who may have THREE TICKETS of ADMISSION to Guildhall, on that day.

Address to W.S. at Mr. Twaites's, Bunch of Grapes, Dowgate-hill.

This day is published,

A PORTRAIT of LORD NELSON, from a Picture painted by J. HOPPNER, R. A. for his Royal Highness the Prince of Wales.

To be had of Messrs. Colnaghi, Cockspur-street, Haymarket, and at the Engraver's, 64, Great Russell-street, Bloomsbury.

WANTED to RENT, for three Months, a small DWELLING-HOUSE, ready furnished, in an airy situation, suitable for the reception of a genteel family, within half an hour's walk West of the Royal Exchange.

Letters (post-paid) addressed to Messrs. Ellis and Fletcher, 26, Fenchurch-street, will be immediately attended to.

LOST, an OLD POINTER DOG, white with red spots, answers to the name of BASTO; almost blind, one eye quite gone.

Any person bringing the said Dog to No. 158, Swallow-street, Piccadilly, shall receive ONE GUINEA Reward, and reasonable expences paid.—N. B. No greater Reward will be offered.

MODERN TOWN COACH and excellent HARNESS.—To be SOLD, an excellent modern TOWN COACH, recently built by Mr. Leader, of Long-Acre, in very good condition, painted dark brown, with harness for a pair of horses, almost new.

Enquire of Messrs. Ellis and Fletcher, 126, Fenchurch-street.

A FINE MARE to be SOLD, the property of a Gentleman, warranted sound; walks, trots, gallops, and leaps remarkably well. To prevent trouble, the price is 40 guineas. Trial allowed.

To be seen at Culuppen's Livery Stables, Coleman-street.

TO be SOLD, an old-established and very complete PACK of well-bred BONY HARRIERS, 20 inches high; also, FOUR capital well-bred HUNTERS, equal to great weights, in good condition, warranted sound, and free from blemish.

Enquire (if by letter post-paid) of Mr. J. Murcott, Warwick-square, Paternoster-row, London.

THE PROPRIETOR of the CITY REPOSITORY, BARBICAN, respectfully informs the Public, that the above Premises continue open for the reception of HORSES, CARRIAGES, HARNESS, &c. for SALE by PUBLIC AUCTION or PRIVATE CONTRACT. The greatest care and attention will be paid, and the utmost of his abilities exerted for the interest of his employers. Horses, &c. should be, if possible, sent in one day prior to the Sale, as they will stand forward, and better to come out. The Public Sale Days are Tuesdays and Fridays, when any Gentleman wishing to purchase are sure of being accommodated, as there are generally about 120 Lots of Horses, &c. on Sale.

N. B. Gentlemen's Studs, Hackneymen, Coach-Masters, Coal-Merchants, Waggon Masters, Town Carmen, and Farmers' Stocks, valued with accuracy, or Sold, either at his Repository, at any part of Town, or in the Country.

MONMOUTHSHIRE.—To be SOLD by PRIVATE CONTRACT, a very desirable FREEHOLD ESTATE, called Gregory Farm, in the Parish of Llanvair Kilgeddin, containing 64A. 1R 34P. of very excellent Arable, Meadow and Pasture Land, with Farm-house and useful Buildings, Yards, Garden, and Orchard, also a Cottage and Garden adjoining the Estate. The whole is in the occupation of Mr. Edward Lewis, tenant at will. The Estate is situated in one of the most beautiful and fertile parts of the county, about 4 miles from the capital Market Town of Abergavenny, and a short distance from the Turnpike-road leading from thence to Usk. There are several flourishing Iron Manufactories in the neighbourhood, and the River Usk, famous for its trout and salmon, runs at a short distance from the land. The land-tax has been redeemed.

For further particulars, apply to Messrs. Barrow, Forbes, and Hancock, Basinghall-street; or Mr. Hogg, Land Surveyor, 34. Castle-street, Holborn.

IRISH LINENS, FRENCH CAMBRICS, &c. wholesale and retail, at No. 55, Oxford-street, corner of Berner's-street.—WM. COOPER has just received several boxes of Irish Linens, particularly cheap; several boxes of French cambrics, very fine, at 50s. the piece, upwards. A large quantity of blankets, counterpains, Marseilles quilts, bed-furnitures, several boxes of damask and diaper table linen, with napkins to match, sheetings of every description very cheap, stout India Calico, full ell-wide, at 12d. and 14d. per yard, with a variety of other articles. As a low wholesale price is invariably asked (being much under the regular price) no abatement is ever made.

THE THREE PIGEONS, 296, Holborn, opposite Brownlow street.—BETTS, real Fur Manufacturer, begs leave to inform the Ladies, and the Public in general, that he has now ready for their inspection, a very extensive ASSORTMENT of MUFFS, TIPPETS, TRIMMINGS for PELISSES, &c. &c. all of his own manufactory, very considerably under the usual prices.—J. B. having purchased a large quantity of Skins at the last March sales, remarkably low, and has had them made up immediately under his own inspection, is enabled to sell full 30 per cent. lower than the trade in general. Velvets for Spencers and Pelisses, from 7s. per yard upwards; Gloves 1s per pair upwards; yard-wide Silk Handkerchiefs 6s. each; Lace and Haberdashery remarkably cheap. A large assortment of Velvet Hats and Bonnets of all descriptions and prices.—J. Betts invites the Ladies, and Public in general, to favour him with a call, having no doubt but he will have it in his power to offer them the above goods at such prices as will secure him a decided preference.

THE ORIGINAL MANUFACTORY.—The frequent attempts to mislead the Public, induces BUTLER to request the Public to be particular as to the house.—The PATENT BEDSTEADS and DINING TABLES only, Catherine-street, Nos. 13 and 14. Also Sofa Beds, Chair Beds and Tables all upon an entire new construction, the superiority, elegance, and convenience of which is generally allowed, as well as their remarkable portability and conveniency in taking down and fixing up. Also an elegant assortment of dining-room, drawing-room, and other chairs, tables, drawers, bed furnitures, window-curtains, &c. with every article for furnishing houses complete, of excellent workmanship, and well seasoned materials. Butler's Patent Articles and improvements in Furniture have been graciously patronized by the King and Queen, their Royal Highnesses the Prince of Wales, Duke of York and Princesses. Butler's Manufactory is a brick front house, Catherine-street, several doors from the Strand. Also for exportation. Navy and Army Equipage.

THEIR MAJESTIES Upholsterers and Cabinet-manufacturers for the Original PATENT BEDSTEADS, SOFA BEDS, and CHAIR BEDS, with very considerable Improvements, by MORGAN and SANDERS, Inventors of their much-admired Imperial Dining Tables and Portable Chairs, and Manufacturers in general of Modern Upholstery and Cabinet Furniture. A very large stock of every article in the above branches are always ready for inspection, for the furnishing houses complete, in the first style of fashion, and warranted of the best workmanship and choicest materials. Elegant 4-post beds and bedding complete, with new designed window-curtains, patent musquito net beds, particularly portable, for all foreign climates, by Morgan and Sanders, Furnishing Upholsterers and Cabinet Manufacturers, No 16 and 17, Catherine-street, Strand. Please to observe, No. 16 and 17, has no connection whatever with any other Warehouse in London. Army and Navy Equipage of every description, on improved principles, very portable.

The LONDON GAZETTE EXTRAORDINARY.

WEDNESDAY, NOV. 6, 1805.

ADMIRALTY-OFFICE, Nov. 6.

Dispatches, of which the following are Copies, were received at the Admiralty this day, at one o'clock A. M. from Vice-Admiral Collingwood, Commander in Chief of his Majesty's ships and vessels off Cadiz:—

SIR, *Euryalus, off Cape Trafalgar, Oct. 22, 1805.*

The ever-to-be-lamented death of Vice-Admiral Lord Viscount Nelson, who, in the late conflict with the enemy, fell in the hour of victory, leaves to me the duty of informing my Lords Commissioners of the Admiralty, that on the 19th instant, it was communicated to the Commander in Chief, from the ships watching the motions of the enemy in Cadiz, that the Combined Fleet had put to sea; as they sailed with light winds westerly, his Lordship concluded their destination was the Mediterranean, and immediately made all sail for the Streights' entrance, with the British Squadron, consisting of twenty-seven ships, three of them sixty-fours, where his Lordship was informed, by Captain Blackwood (whose vigilance in watching, and giving notice of the enemy's movements, has been highly meritorious), that they had not yet passed the Streights.

On Monday the 21st instant, at day-light, when Cape Trafalgar bore E. by S. about seven leagues, the enemy was discovered six or seven miles to the Eastward, the wind about West, and very light; the Commander in Chief immediately made the signal for the fleet to bear up in two columns, as they are formed in order of sailing; a mode of attack his Lordship had previously directed, to avoid the inconvenience and delay in forming a line of battle in the usual manner. The enemy's line consisted of thirty-three ships (of which eighteen were French, and fifteen Spanish), commanded in Chief by Admiral Villeneuve: the Spaniards, under the direction of Gravina, wore, with their heads to the Northward, and formed their line of battle with great closeness and correctness; but as the mode of attack was unusual, so the structure of their line was new; it formed a crescent, convexing to leeward, so that, in leading down to their centre, I had both their van and rear abaft the beam; before the fire opened, every alternate ship was about a cable's length to windward of her second a-head and a-stern, forming a kind of double line, and appeared, when on their beam, to leave a very little interval between them; and this without crowding their ships. Admiral Villeneuve was in the Bucentaure, in the centre, and the Prince of Asturias bore Gravina's flag in the rear, but the French and Spanish ships were mixed without any apparent regard to order of national squadron.

As the mode of our attack had been previously determined on, and communicated to the Flag-Officers, and Captains, few signals were necessary, and none were made, except to direct close order as the lines bore down.

The Commander in Chief, in the Victory, led the weather column, and the Royal Sovereign, which bore my flag, the lee.

The action began at twelve o'clock, by the leading ships of the columns breaking through the enemy's line, the Commander in Chief about the tenth ship from the van, the Second in Command about the twelfth from the rear, leaving the van of the enemy unoccupied; the succeeding ships breaking through, in all parts, astern of their leaders, and engaging the enemy at the muzzles of their guns; the conflict was severe; the enemy's ships were fought with a gallantry highly honourable to their Officers; but the attack on them was irresistible, and it pleased the Almighty Disposer of all events to grant his Majesty's arms a complete and glorious victory. About three P. M. many of the enemy's ships having struck their colours, their line gave way; Admiral Gravina, with ten ships joining their frigates to leeward, stood towards Cadiz. The five headmost ships in their van tacked, and standing to the Southward, to windward of the British line, were engaged, and the sternmost of them taken; the others went off, leaving to his Majesty's squadron nineteen ships of the line (of which two are first rates, the Santissima Trinidad and the Santa Anna,) with three Flag Officers, viz. Admiral Villeneuve, the Commander in Chief; Don Ignatio Maria D'Aliva, Vice Admiral; and the Spanish Rear-Admiral, Don Baltazar Hidalgo Cisneros.

After such a Victory, it may appear unnecessary to enter into encomiums on the particular parts taken by the several Commanders; the conclusion says more on the subject than I have language to express; the spirit which animated all was the same: when all exert themselves zealously in their country's service, all deserve that their high merits should stand recorded; and never was high merit more conspicuous than in the battle I have described.

The Achille (a French 74), after having surrendered, by some mismanagement of the Frenchmen, took fire and blew up; two hundred of her men were saved by the Tenders.

A circumstance occurred during the action, which so strongly marks the invincible spirit of British seamen, when engaging the enemies of their country, that I cannot resist the pleasure I have in making it known to their Lordships; the Temeraire was boarded by accident, or design, by a French ship on one side, and a Spaniard on the other; the contest was vigorous, but, in the end, the Combined Ensigns were torn from the poop, and the British hoisted in their places.

Such a battle could not be fought without sustaining a great loss of men. I have not only to lament, in common with the British Navy, and the British Nation, in the Fall of the Commander in Chief, the loss of a Hero, whose name will be immortal, and his memory ever dear to his country; but my heart is rent with the most poignant grief for the death of a friend, to whom, by many years intimacy, and a perfect knowledge of the virtues of his mind, which inspired ideas superior to the common race of men, I was bound by the strongest ties of affection; a grief to which even the glorious occasion in which he fell, does not bring the consolation which, perhaps, it ought: his Lordship received a musket ball in his left breast, about the middle of the action, and sent an Officer to me immediately with his last farewell; and soon after expired.

I have also to lament the loss of those excellent Officers, Captains Duff, of the Mars, and Cooke, of the Bellerophon; I have yet heard of none others.

I fear the numbers that have fallen will be found very great, when the returns come to me; but it having blown a gale of wind ever since the action, I have not yet had it in my power to collect any reports from the ships.

The Royal Sovereign having lost her masts, except the tottering foremast, I called the Euryalus to me, while the action continued, which ship lying within hail, made my signals—a service Captain Blackwood performed with great attention: after the action, I shifted my flag to her, that I might more easily communicate any orders to, and collect the ships, and towed the Royal Sovereign out to Seaward. The whole fleet were now in a very perilous situation, many dismasted, all shattered, in thirteen fathom water, off the shoals of Trafalgar; and when I made the signal to prepare to anchor, few of the ships had an anchor to let go, their cables being shot; but the same good Providence which aided us through such a day preserved us in the night, by the wind shifting a few points, and drifting the ships off the land, except four of the captured dismasted ships, which are now at anchor off Trafalgar, and I hope will ride safe until those gales are over.

Having thus detailed the proceedings of the fleet on this occasion, I beg to congratulate their Lordships on a victory which, I hope, will add a ray to the glory of his Majesty's crown, and be attended with public benefit to our country. I am, &c.

(Signed) C. COLLINGWOOD.

William Marsden, Esq.

The order in which the Ships of the British Squadron attacked the Combined Fleets, on the 21st of October, 1805.

VAN.	REAR.
Victory,	Royal Sovereign,
Temeraire,	Mars,
Neptune,	Belleisle,
Conqueror,	Tonnant,
Leviathan,	Bellerophon,
Ajax,	Colossus,
Orion,	Achille,
Agamemnon,	Polyphemus,
Minotaur,	Revenge,
Spartiate,	Swiftsure,
Britannia,	Defence,
Africa,	Thunderer,
Euryalus,	Defiance,
Sirius,	Prince,
Phœbe,	Dreadnought.
Naiad,	
Pickle Schooner,	
Entreprenante Cutter.	

(Signed) C. COLLINGWOOD.

GENERAL ORDER.

Euryalus, October 22, 1805.

The ever-to-be-lamented death of Lord Viscount Nelson, Duke of Bronté, the Commander in Chief, who fell in the action of the twenty-first, in the arms of victory, covered with glory; whose memory will be ever dear to the British Navy, and the British Nation; whose zeal for the honour of his King, and for the interests of his Country, will be ever held up as a shining example for a British Seaman—leaves to me a duty to return my thanks to the Right Honourable Rear-Admiral, the Captains, Officers, Seamen, and detachments of Royal Marines serving on board his Majesty's Squadron now under my command, for their conduct on that day; but where can I find language to express my sentiments of the valour and skill which were displayed by the Officers the Seamen, and Marines in the battle with the enemy, where every individual appeared an Hero, on whom the Glory of his Country depended; the attack was irresistible, and the issue of it adds to the page of Naval Annals a brilliant instance of what Britons can do, when their King and their Country need their service.

To the Right Honourable Rear-Admiral the Earl of Northesk, to the Captains, Officers, and Seamen and to the Officers, Non-commissioned Officers, and Privates of the Royal Marines, I beg to give my sincere and hearty thanks for their highly meritorious conduct, both in the action, and in their zeal and activity in bringing the captured ships out from the perilous situation in which they were after their surrender, among the shoals of Trafalgar, in boisterous weather.

And I desire that the respective Captains will be pleased to communicate to the Officers, Seamen, and Royal Marines, this public testimony of my high approbation of their conduct, and my thanks for it. (Signed) C. COLLINGWOOD

To the Right Honourable Rear-Admiral the Earl of Northesk, and the respective Captains and Commanders.

GENERAL ORDER.

The Almighty God, whose arm is strength, having of his great mercy been pleased to crown the exertion of his Majesty's fleet with success, in giving them a complete victory over their enemies, on 21st of this month; and that all praise and thanksgiving may be offered up to the Throne of Grace for the great benefits to our country and to mankind:

I have thought proper, that a day should be appointed of general humiliation before God, and thanksgiving for this his merciful goodness, imploring forgiveness of sins, a continuation of his divine mercy, and his constant aid to us, in the defence of our country's liberties and laws, without which the utmost efforts of man are nought; and direct, therefore, that be appointed for this holy purpose.

Given on board the Euryalus, off Cape Trafalgar, 22d Oct. 1805

(Signed) C. COLLINGWOOD.

To the respective Captains and Commanders.

N. B. The fleet having been dispersed by a gale of wind, no day has yet been able to be appointed for the above purpose.

SIR, *Euryalus, off Cadiz, Oct. 24, 1805.*

In my letter of the 22d, I detailed to you, for the information of my Lords Commissioners of the Admiralty, the proceedings of his Majesty's squadron on the day of the action, and that preceding it, since which I have had a continued series of misfortunes; but they are of a kind that human prudence could not possibly provide against, or my skill prevent.

On the 22d, in the morning, a strong southerly wind blew, with squally weather, which, however, did not prevent the activity of the Officers and Seamen of such ships as were manageable, from getting hold of many of the prizes (thirteen or fourteen), and towing them off to the Westward, where I ordered them to rendezvous round the Royal Sovereign, in tow by the Neptune: but on the 23d the gale increased, and the sea ran so high that many of them broke the tow-rope, and drifted far to leeward before they were got hold of again; and some of them, taking advantage in the dark and boisterous night, got before the wind, and have, perhaps, drifted upon the shore and sunk; on the afternoon of that day the remnant of the Combined Fleet, ten sail of ships, who had not been much engaged, stood up to leeward of my shattered and straggled charge, as if meaning to attack them, which obliged me to collect a force out of the least injured ships, and form to leeward for their defence; all this retarded the progress of the hulks, and the bad weather continuing, determined me to destroy all the leewardmost that could be cleared of the men, considering that keeping possession of the ships was a matter of little consequence, compared with the chance of their falling again into the hands of the enemy; but even this was an arduous task in the high sea which was running. I hope, however, it has been accomplished to a considerable extent; I entrusted it to skilful Officers, who would spare no pains to execute what was possible. The Captains of the Prince and Neptune cleared the Trinidad and sunk her Captains Hope, Bayntun, and Malcolm, who joined the fleet this moment from Gibraltar, had the charge of destroying four others. The Redoubtable sunk astern of the Swiftsure while in tow. The Santa Anna, I have no doubt, is sunk, as her side was almost entirely beat in; and such is the shattered condition of the whole of them, that unless the weather moderates I doubt whether I shall be able to carry a ship of them into port. I hope their Lordships will approve of what I (having only in consideration the destruction of the enemy's fleet) have thought a measure of absolute necessity.

I have taken Admiral Villeneuve into this ship; Vice-Admiral Don Aliva is dead. Whenever the temper of the weather will permit, and I can spare a frigate (for there were only four in the action with the fleet, Euryalus, Sirius, Phœbe, and Naiad; the Melpomene joined the 22d, and the Eurydice and Scout the 23d,) I shall collect the other flag officers, and send them to England, with their flags, if they do not all go to the bottom), to be laid at his Majesty's feet.

There were four thousand troops embarked, under

having early in her marriage, from the want of other employment, and the circumstance of Sir Thomas's being in Parliament, got into the way of making and keeping correspondents, and formed for herself a very creditable, common-place, amplifying style, so that a very little matter was enough for her.

(*MP*, 44)

A woman may not, however, write to whom she pleases—a correspondence is almost a contract, not lightly undertaken even between coevals and close friends, like Elizabeth Bennet and Charlotte Lucas, or Fanny Price and Mary Crawford. The rule that underlies almost all the novels is one Jane Austen never troubles to expound: that a young woman may not carry on a correspondence with a man, unless she is engaged to him. The difficulty crops up decisively in *Emma*; several of the clues to the secret engagement between Jane Fairfax and Frank Churchill are supplied by hints of a correspondence between them: one when a casual dinner-party conversation brings to light that Jane insists on personally fetching the household's letters from the post office (where they were delivered by the mail-coach), even if it means going out in the rain; and another when it appears that Frank Churchill has heard news that, apparently, no-one has told him. Such hints should suggest that each has a secret correspondent, that the correspondent must be the betrothed, and that the discovery of the correspondence is discovery of the betrothal. The same rule makes Elinor Dashwood take it as certain, when Marianne writes to Willoughby, 'that however mysteriously they might conduct the affair, they must be engaged' (*SS*, 25). Jane Austen's sense of propriety seems to get stronger as she grows older. In *Northanger Abbey*, Catherine's parents will not allow her to become officially engaged to Henry Tilney until his father consents, but 'whenever Catherine received a letter, as, at that time, happened pretty often, they always looked another way' (*NA*, 31). But Anne Elliot in *Persuasion*, when Frederick Wentworth proposes by letter, is perplexed how to get a message to him, and apparently never considers writing a reply. When we know the rules, it becomes suddenly a weighty thing for Edmund to promise to write to Fanny at Portsmouth from Mansfield, even though she is his cousin, and even though in it he will tell her that he is to marry another woman.

The letter itself at this period looked different from a modern
one. Letters were paid for by the recipient, on delivery, and
charged by weight. The only exception is that M.P.'s could 'frank'
letters, which then went through the post free of charge. A letter
therefore usually consisted of a single sheet of paper with no
envelope, which was folded for addressing and sending, rather
like the modern air-letter, and fastened with sealing-wax. Since
extra paper meant extra cost, letters were often 'crossed': that is,
each sheet, after being written on horizontally, was given a
ninety-degree turn and written over again, in lines running at

A 'crossed' letter, from Fanny Brawne to her fiancé John Keats.

right angles to the first ones. A good clear hand was needed if such a letter was to be decipherable, as Miss Bates deciphers Jane's in *Emma*:

> '[my mother] often says, when the letter is first opened, "Well, Hetty, now I think you will be put to it to make out all that chequer-work." '

$(E, 19)$

Since the receiver paid, the news in it must be worth having, encouraging perhaps a reasonably high standard of letter-writing. The longest letter in the novels is one that does not go by post, nor is it written to a fiancée—Darcy's famous letter to Elizabeth, defending himself from her charges against him. It consists of 'an envelope containing two sheets of letter paper, written quite through, in a very close hand. The envelope itself was likewise full' *(PP,* 35). This 'envelope' is a third sheet of paper, folded as already explained. Jane Austen always gets such details right, but anyone who makes the experiment of getting Darcy's four-thousand-word letter onto six sides of paper, even crossed, will realise how close the writing must have been.

That the basic pattern of the day into which all these affairs fit themselves is a good one is proved by its being convenient to almost all classes—from small tenant farmers up to the aristocracy. Though there are undoubtedly different ways of managing the daily round, even in Jane Austen's time, notably in the new and fast-growing industrial towns in the Midlands and the North, this way suits a civilisation, as the eighteenth century was, which is founded upon a way of life lived in the country, in which the town is not, for most people, home, and in a society which, while undoubtedly having class divisions, was flexible in its operation and attitude to them. England, as historians point out, has no aristocracy as France had, whose ranks might not be entered from below, nor has it, strictly speaking, a peasantry either.

People with very different degrees of prosperity and intellect living together, in fairly close contact, must have a code by which to do so. The eighteenth-century code of manners is a fairly strict one, both between social groups and within them. Between different classes the rules and distinctions are usually so broad as to be obvious; but within a smaller social group such as Jane Austen handles, the discriminations are much less obvious to the reader to whom they are no longer as natural as they were to Jane Austen and her contemporaries.

Manners in Jane Austen's novels are a great deal more formal and less free than today. They are one of her most vital ways of interpreting characters, whose misbehaviour, and small fallings-off from proper behaviour, may point to more important moral faults. Plainly Jane Austen does not stop to explain bad or faulty manners that she assumes all her readers will recognise, and a modern reader can stray badly in his response if he does not notice when decorum is being offended.

Formality is noticeable immediately in modes of address. Husbands and wives refer to each other as 'Mr' and 'Mrs', both when speaking to each other and to third parties—a custom which pervades all the novels. The 'my dear Mr Bennet' of his wife in *Pride and Prejudice* is almost a comic catch-phrase, but the sensible Mrs Weston in *Emma* is equally precise in referring to her husband. Mr Knightley and Emma herself, who are perhaps the closest *friends* among all Jane Austen's pairs of lovers, are the only ones to discuss the matter—he of course calls her by her Christian name because he has known her since she was a child:

> ' "Mr Knightley."—You always called me, "Mr Knightley;" and, from habit it has not so very formal a sound.—And yet it is formal. I want you to call me something else, but I do not know what.'
>
> 'I remember once calling you "George," in one of my amiable fits, about ten years ago. I did it because I thought it would offend you; but, as you made no objection, I never did it again.'
>
> 'And cannot you call me "George" now?'
>
> 'Impossible!—I never can call you anything but "Mr Knightley." I will not promise to equal even the elegant terseness of Mrs Elton, by calling you Mr K.'
>
> (*E.* 53)

Mrs Elton, to whom Emma alludes, having exhibited her vulgarity of manners and mind in many ways, exhibits them also by referring to her husband as 'Mr E.'.

Age and seniority count for a great deal in formality. Parents are generally 'sir', and 'ma'am' or 'madam', to their children, so that the reader ought to notice the extra affection and familiarity when Emma calls Mr Woodhouse 'papa'. Jane Austen herself in letters, even to her sister, invariably refers to '*my* mother' and makes fun of a servant who merely refers to 'mother'.[1] Within the same generation age demands respect: Jane Bennet, the eldest of the family of five daughters in *Pride and Prejudice*, is Miss Bennet; Elizabeth is properly Miss Elizabeth, and when Miss Bingley calls her Miss Eliza she is being both disrespectful and rude. Fanny Price, cousin to the Bertram family of Mansfield Park, has lived with them long enough to be almost a sister, but still refers to the eldest as Mr and Miss Bertram, not Tom and Maria. Seniority is carefully observed even when it would seem to be unnecessary, as a natural matter of decorum. Since John Dashwood in *Sense and Sensibility* is of the next generation to his stepmother Mrs Dashwood, his wife is invariably Mrs *John* Dashwood; similarly, since Emma's sister Isabella is married to a younger brother, she is not Mrs Knightley, but Mrs John Knightley, even though the elder Mr Knightley is not married. When the elder brother is away, though, the Christian name may be omitted. Mary Crawford rejoices when Tom Bertram goes away from Mansfield Park:

'I am so glad your eldest cousin is gone that [Edmund] *may* be Mr Bertram again. There is something in the sound of Mr *Edmund* Bertram so formal, so pitiful, so younger-brother-like, that I detest it.'

(*MP*, 22)

Social position is the other great decider of forms of address. The mother of Tom and Maria, Lady Bertram, wife of a baronet, calls her sister Mrs Norris—a clergyman's widow—simply 'sister'; but Mrs Norris in her turn, although the elder of the two, invariably uses 'Lady Bertram' to one who is now her social superior. Mrs Norris is a snob, and so is a useful guide on what is dear to her heart; she speaks of her grown-up nieces as 'dear Julia and dearest Mrs Rushworth', even though she has known them from babies, because Maria, now Mrs Rushworth, has aggrandised herself by a noble marriage. In the respect due to rank Mrs Elton is the novels' greatest offender, and seldom puts a foot right. As well as being vulgar, she over-rates her own position, and is therefore always

[1] Letter to Cassandra Austen, Tuesday 24 January 1809.

too familiar and informal, whether calling her husband 'Mr E.', or speaking to Mr Knightley simply as 'Knightley', or of *Jane* Fairfax when she should say Miss Fairfax. 'Heavens! [is Emma's reaction] Let me not suppose that she dares go about, Emma Woodhouse-ing me!—But upon my honour, there seem no limits to the licentiousness of that woman's tongue!' (*E*, 33).

Christian names in general are used very sparingly, even among young people, relations, and friends. One can see in *Sense and Sensibility* that it is a mark of exceptional intimacy in Mrs John Dashwood that she 'called Lucy by her Christian name' (*SS*, 35). Even quite close friends of the same age can remain formal, like Fanny Price and Mary Crawford who, although they see a good deal of each other at Mansfield, do not use Christian names until Mary thinks that Fanny is engaged to her brother, and may thus be treated as a sister, when she begins her letter with 'MY DEAR FANNY, for so I may now always call you, to the infinite relief of a tongue that has been stumbling at *Miss Price* for at least the last six weeks' (*MP*, 31).

To confuse the modern reader further, there are some differences in manners between the early three novels—*Northanger Abbey*, *Sense and Sensibility*, and *Pride and Prejudice*[1]—and the later three—*Mansfield Park*, *Emma*, and *Persuasion*—particularly in the way women address men. In *Sense and Sensibility* and *Pride and Prejudice*, Willoughby, Wickham, Darcy and Bingley, and other young men generally, are commonly mentioned in conversation without the title 'Mr', without any feeling that those who mention them are as deplorable as Mrs Elton referring to Knightley. Even so, while Marianne Dashwood, all sensibility, calls her lover 'Willoughby', Elinor's good sense may be detected when she invariably calls hers '*Mr* Ferrars'.

Decorum of behaviour is as pervasive, and as little stressed, as decorum of address—only to be registered by the reader when significant, or when violated. Jane Austen recognises that rank has its claims—that the immortally silly clergyman Mr Collins in *Pride and Prejudice* should not introduce himself to the distinguished Mr Darcy, but wait for a first move from Mr Darcy—but she

---

[1] Although the six novels were all published within ten years, the early group were all written—or at least existed in some form—many years before.

shows no respect for meaningless subservience, or snobbery: Mr Collins is equally ridiculous in his excessive and servile humility to his patron Lady Catherine de Bourgh. In her later work, *Persuasion*, Sir Walter Elliot, himself a baronet, degrades himself by his servile enthusiasm for a dowager viscountess. Jane Austen derides artificial and pointless conventions, like the rigid distinction between girls who are 'out' in society, and their younger sisters who are 'not out', and to be treated as children who are still finishing their education. Mary Crawford, visiting Mansfield Park from London, is the voice of such conventions:

> 'I begin now to understand you all, except Miss Price,' said Miss Crawford, as she was walking with the Mr Bertrams. 'Pray, is she out, or is she not?—I am puzzled.—She dined at the parsonage, with the rest of you, which seemed like being *out*; and yet she says so little, that I can hardly suppose she *is*.'
>
> Edmund, to whom this was chiefly addressed, replied, 'I believe I know what you mean—but I will not undertake to answer the question. My cousin is grown up. She has the age and sense of a woman, but the outs and not outs are beyond me.'
>
> 'And yet in general, nothing can be more easily ascertained. The distinction is so broad. Manners as well as appearance are, generally speaking, so totally different. Till now, I could not have supposed it possible to be mistaken as to a girl's being out or not. A girl not out, has always the same sort of dress; a close bonnet for instance, looks very demure, and never says a word. You may smile—but it is so I assure you—and except that it is sometimes carried a little too far, it is all very proper.'
>
> (*MP*, 5)

Quite plainly Edmund's is the good sense here, not Mary's. Jane Austen has even earlier, in *Pride and Prejudice*, condemned the convention that the younger girls in a family must wait for the elder to be married before they can enter society; Elizabeth Bennet replies sharply to Lady Catherine de Bourgh:

> 'I think it would be very hard upon younger sisters, that they should not have their share of society and amusement because the elder may not have the means or inclination to marry early.—The last born has as good a right to the pleasures of youth, as the first. And to be kept back on *such* a motive!—I think it would not be likely to promote sisterly affection or delicacy of mind.'
>
> (*PP*, 29)

Jane Austen is no egalitarian; she accepts distinctions of rank whose conventions can cause no such damage. Elizabeth Elliot in *Persuasion* has, as eldest daughter of a baronet,

> been doing the honours and laying down the domestic law at home, and leading the way to the chaise and four, and walking immediately after Lady Russell out of all the drawing-rooms and dining-rooms in the country. Thirteen winters had seen her opening every ball of credit which a scanty neighbourhood afforded.
>
> (*P*, 1)

The last duty, one that falls upon Fanny Price when her cousins are away from Mansfield Park, is one that she, shy as she is, acknowledges as proper:

> She must submit, as her own propriety of mind directed, in spite of Aunt Norris's opinion, to being the principal lady in the company, and to all the little distinctions consequent thereon.
>
> (*MP*, 23)

When, in *Emma*, Mrs Elton claims similar distinctions, what is wrong is not that, as the leading married woman in Highbury society, she takes precedence, but that she makes so much fuss about it:

> Dinner was on the table.—Mrs Elton, before she could be spoken to, was ready; and before Mr Woodhouse had reached her with his request to be allowed to hand her into the dining parlour, was saying—
> 'Must I go first? I really am ashamed of always leading the way.'
>
> (*E*, 34)

Although Mrs Elton calls herself the chaperone of the Box Hill party, being the only married woman there, the chaperone system is not yet what it later became, particularly in the middle classes: rigid, artificial, and silly. In Jane Austen's society young men and women may be together without any appointed third party to see that they behave themselves: Marianne Dashwood in *Sense and Sensibility* can ride out in Willoughby's carriage, Catherine Morland in *Northanger Abbey* can ride in John Thorpe's, and Elizabeth Bennet and Darcy in *Pride and Prejudice* may walk. Even so, it is clear that the sensible young woman avoids the *tête à tête* where it will cause remark. Marianne in the first example is deliberately flouting what she feels to be excessive and artificial prudence; while, in the second example, Mr Allen, *in loco parentis*, warns Catherine that while, 'as far as it has gone hitherto, there is no harm done' yet 'These schemes are not at all the thing. Young men and women driving about the country in open carriages! Now and then it is very well; but going to inns and public places together! It is not right' (*NA*, 14).

One does not feel many restrictions on women that do not have a basis in common prudence. One that might be mentioned concerns the habit of walking unaccompanied. When Elizabeth Bennet walks three miles 'alone, quite alone' (*PP*, 8) Miss Bingley is shocked, but she is plainly no-one whom the reader much respects, and there has been no great offence against propriety. However, Emma does not like going out by herself, even half a mile—'She had ventured once alone to Randalls, but it was not pleasant' (*E*, 4)—and when her friend Harriet, in the same novel, is assailed by gipsies, Jane Austen feels it necessary to give her a companion on her walk, Miss Bickerton, whom her author then has to get rid of so that Frank Churchill can romantically rescue the lone and beleaguered Harriet.

Embargos on subjects for conversation on the other hand are not at all noticeable, nor, even on close scrutiny, are there many of them. Only from *Northanger Abbey* can we establish the rule that politics are not a subject for women:

> Henry suffered the subject to decline, and by an easy transition from a piece of rocky fragment and the withered oak which he had placed near its summit, to oaks in general, to forests, the inclosure of them, waste lands, crown lands and government, he shortly found himself arrived at politics; and from politics, it was an easy step to silence.
>
> (*NA*, 14)

While there are many fine discriminations to be made—that a reader must make, because they reveal attitudes and thereby character and morals, which are based upon the very words speakers use—hardly any actual topics are offered for objection on grounds merely of refinement or decorum. Characters who do thus object are even revealed as foolish ones, like Lady Middleton in *Sense and Sensibility*, who cannot bear her mother's mention of pregnancy:

> 'I wanted her to stay at home and rest this morning, but she would come with us; she longed so much to see you all!'
>
> Mrs Palmer laughed, and said it would not do her any harm.
>
> 'She expects to be confined in February,' continued Mrs Jennings.
>
> Lady Middleton could no longer endure such a conversation, and therefore exerted herself to ask Mr Palmer if there was any news in the paper.
>
> (*SS*, 20)

Colonel Brandon, in the same novel, can explain to Elinor, a girl of nineteen, a whole history of seduction, illegitimacy, and desertion; in *Pride and Prejudice*, Elizabeth Bennet, forced to tell Darcy that her sister Lydia is living unmarried with Wickham, feels shame and distress at admitting her sister's disgrace and family's misery, but none at having to find the words to do it. Prudery has no part in Jane Austen's reticences, and, while the outspoken frankness of the Georgians is not hers, neither is Victorian primness.

Private conversations can be had, paradoxically, more easily in large groups than anywhere else, with less danger of exciting gossip or of being interrupted. Such conversations would be even easier than now, and some of what seem to be the improbabilities of these, quite numerous, private exchanges disappear when one remembers that rooms in such houses as Jane Austen's characters inhabit were fairly large, that music and other talk both drown talk, and that candlelight divides a room into areas of light and shadow. Jane Austen appreciates, and uses, the force of all these things. In *Sense and Sensibility*, Elinor Dashwood can listen to the most confidential, and unwelcome, exposures from Lucy Steele, without the least danger of being overheard:

> The piano-forte, at which Marianne, wrapt up in her own music and her own thoughts, had by this time forgotten that any body was in the room beside herself, was luckily so near them that Miss Dashwood now judged she might safely, under the shelter of its noise, introduce the interesting subject, without any risk of being heard at the card-table.
>
> (*SS*, 24)

In *Mansfield Park*, dusk and a pianoforte are more delicately used:

> Miss Crawford was standing at an open window with Edmund and Fanny looking out on a twilight scene, while the Miss Bertrams, Mr Rushworth, and Henry Crawford, were all busy with candles at the pianoforte.
>
> (*MP*, 11)

Mary expostulates with Edmund on his decision to become a clergyman, then when she leaves them to take her turn at the piano, Edmund and Fanny, left in the shadows, can talk about her, and about the stars and the night sky, as if quite alone.

Courtship nevertheless is somewhat public, with a third person present at most of the important interviews between Jane Austen's young people. In *Mansfield Park*, Fanny is an unwilling spectator while Mary Crawford and Edmund rehearse the important scene from the play *Lover's Vows*, a scene in which the young woman virtually proposes to the man—when, as anyone familiar with the play[1] will agree, Mary and Edmund might well wish to have an observer, to dissipate some of the embarrassment. But later in the same novel, when Fanny in her turn is visited by Henry Crawford at Portsmouth, her younger sister Susan is a sharer in their conversations: 'He could have wished her sister away. A quick looking girl of Susan's age was the very worst third in the world' (*MP*, 41). It is only by accident or by careful contrivance of accident that a private interview can occur, as when Charlotte Lucas 'perceived [Mr Collins] from an upper window as he walked towards the house, and instantly set out to meet him accidentally in the lane' (*PP*, 22). Elizabeth Bennet at Hunsford happens to stay at home with a headache while her hosts dine out, so Darcy seizes the chance to see her alone and make his first, disastrous, proposal of marriage; Mr Elton, making an even more disastrous one to Emma, is lucky that

> John Knightley, forgetting that he did not belong to the [first coach's] party, stept in after his wife very naturally; so that Emma found, on being escorted and followed into the second carriage by Mr Elton, that the door was to be lawfully shut on them, and that they were to have a tête-à-tête drive.
>
> (*E*, 15)

---

[1] It is printed as an appendix to *Mansfield Park*, in R. W. Chapman's edition, Oxford.

Emma does not mind, because she thinks she can talk to him about Harriet, with whom she supposes him in love; and equally it is perfectly in order for Captain Wentworth, in *Persuasion*, to escort Anne Elliot home when she has a headache—he, however, has already proposed, and Anne, accepting the walk, accepts also the man.

The *tête-à-tête*, clearly, is not wrong; but there is little place in social everyday life for a man and woman to be alone together, even after they are married, nor is it considered as necessary as it is today. The only character who has a honeymoon in the modern sense is Emma, who contrives 'a fortnight's absence in a tour to the seaside' (*E*, 55), while her sister looks after her father. But Maria Bertram in *Mansfield Park*, marrying money and an estate, goes straight to that estate from the church door, and takes her younger sister with her. Elizabeth Bennet, looking happily forward to her married life, anticipates company as one of the pleasures of 'the time when they should be removed from society so little pleasing to either [herself or Darcy], to all the comfort and elegance of their family party at Pemberley' (*PP*, 60)—the family party comprising Darcy's young sister Georgiana, and Elizabeth's sister Kitty. In any case, young children soon arrive to enlarge family parties, and long visits between relations add to such social living.

CHAPTER THREE

The Common Task

Within the framework of the day, the duties of life are performed, from the cradle to the grave. Many more of these duties could be carried out actually within the home and the domestic circle at the opening of the nineteenth century than can be in the twentieth, for all classes of society, but particularly for the gentry who are Jane Austen's first concern. She is but little occupied with the cradle, and less with the grave. Her emphasis is on the most interesting, influential, and vigorous years of life, when her major characters, all young people, are shaping their natures, and ordering their lives; and when her minor ones, young and middle-aged, are appreciating the consequences of choices made before the novels began, or while they are proceeding. Her characters, in fact, are seen in the process of using what nature and education have bestowed upon them, so it is necessary to perceive what kind of education is being offered. Learning as such is plainly esteemed, not only for its practical value but as a necessary part of worth, gentility, and breeding. Jane Austen does not dwell much upon the actual processes of learning, being more concerned with chronicling what her characters do with it; she drops allusions only when they are relevant to situation, and depends upon her reader to supply details from his own knowledge.

Very small children are the combined care of parents, but in particular the mother, and whatever nursemaids her income may allow. Small children, once of an age to learn, do so at home. Day schools are only for working-class children; the families in Jane Austen's novels have governesses if they can afford them, as Mr Woodhouse provides the invaluable Miss Taylor for his daughters Isabella and Emma; or if they cannot, the main burden of teaching falls upon the parents. In a parsonage such as that of Catherine Morland's parents, in *Northanger Abbey*, Mrs Morland, as well as running the household, teaches her eleven children successively to read, write, and number, as Catherine tells Henry Tilney:

> 'If you had been as much used as myself to hear poor little children first learning their letters and then learning to spell, if you had ever seen how stupid they can be for a whole morning together, and how tired my poor mother is at the end of it, as I am in the habit of seeing almost every day of my life at home, you would allow that to *torment* and to *instruct* might sometimes be used as synonimous [sic] words.'

(NA, 14)

Her eldest daughter's opinion here shows a feeling balance of sympathies, and reveals the unromantic opposite of the idealising phrases that have formed part of her own education; that it is a

delightful task
To teach the young idea how to shoot.

After such rudimentary beginnings modes of education vary. It is suggested that in such a family as Catherine's, education is mainly what the individual chooses to teach herself; such it is in Elizabeth Bennet's, although they have enough money to do better, and could have employed a governess: Lady Catherine demands,

> 'Then, who taught you? who attended to you? Without a governess you must have been neglected.'
>
> 'Compared with some families, I believe we were; but such of us as wished to learn, never wanted the means. We were always encouraged to read, and had all the masters that were necessary. Those who chose to be idle, certainly might.'

(PP, 29)

Though the means depend on inclination and status, education is essentially the learning of facts by heart, combined with wide reading to develop taste and judgement. Jane Austen herself and her elder sister Cassandra went to a boarding school. But school is not the usual or even the best way of being educated, for boys up to public school age, or for girls at any age.

The schooling of boys follows the clearest pattern. They begin with a private tutor who, if the family is prosperous enough, lives with the family—a state of affairs that never occurs in the novels—

The school-room at Eton.

or the boy himself may call on, or live with, the tutor. The tutor was often a clergyman who needed pupils as a way of adding to an inadequate income. Jane Austen's father taught boys in this way, alongside his own sons. In the novels, the only male character who goes to a tutor (that we hear of) is the hero of *Sense and Sensibility*, Edward Ferrars. The plan proved a bad one for him, since he had no good company, and contracted his shackling engagement to Lucy Steele, the niece of his tutor. Edward Ferrars is rather unusual (for the eldest son of a rich woman) since he is a youth at the time, whereas the tutor usually instructs younger boys who, having been grounded by him in Greek and Latin (which formed the bulk of their curriculum), would then go on to one of the public schools, the most notable of course being Harrow and Eton. Hair-raising accounts of these schools abound, of the conditions and the startling lack of discipline at them. Since boys of this age do not appear in Jane Austen's novels, she does not refer to such circumstances, but some such experiences must be assumed to have been the lot of many of her young men, and her older ones, and have gone to the making of such excellent persons as Mr Knightley, Mr Darcy, and Edmund Bertram. A young man's education generally, though not always, concludes with the university, meaning either Oxford or Cambridge, the only two English ones then in existence. Here also discipline is negligible, and the quality of the learning, still based upon the classics, dubious. Until the first half of the nineteenth century, modern subjects at Eton were unconnected with the general business of the school, and were attended at extra hours. At Harrow, mathematics did not become a compulsory study until 1837, with modern languages, English history, and English literature being added even later. The egregiously stupid Mr Collins's experience is significantly put:

> 'though he belonged to one of the universities, he had merely kept the necessary terms, *without forming at it any useful acquaintance* [my italics].'
> *(PP, 15)*

The university could very easily be a place where a young man could amuse himself with other young men, cultivate all the fashionable pleasures, and waste a great deal of money. The experience of actual men, such as Wordsworth and Byron at Cambridge, bears out the view Jane Austen gives, that the

Worcester College, Oxford.

Two 'bang-up Oxonians'. *Left*, a Bachelor of Arts, and *right*, a Master of Arts.

universities of England at this period, though learning may be found in them, do not place much of it before the undergraduate. Jane Austen's frankest, and utterly convincing, instance of the power of Oxford *not* to educate a man, is John Thorpe in *Northanger Abbey*. His enthusiasms are horses, carriages, and drink, for which passions he seems to have found full opportunity in a university career. He has learned to brag, bet, and swear; his follies seem to have been left as they were. He is living the life of the 'bang-up Oxonian' (as a contemporary termed him) who was already by 1821 'a species . . . almost extinct'.[1]

[1] Bishop Whateley, *The Quarterly Review*, January 1821.

All clergymen must of course have been to university before they can be ordained, but other young men may find other ways of entering the world. In Jane Austen we do not reach the level of prosperity that sees the Grand Tour of Europe as an alternative mode of completing the education of a gentleman, in which the young man, accompanied by a tutor, studies the life and manners, the languages, the cultural, literary, architectural, and artistic remains of the great cities of Europe. The other openings Jane Austen alludes to are rather training in the professions, like the worthless Mr Wickham's brief attendance at the Inns of Court, in preparation for entering the law, or early admission to the navy, as a means of education and of entry into an honourable profession, for a young man with few resources, like Fanny Price's brother William in *Mansfield Park*.

Though the matter of education seems sparse enough—not much more than a mechanical knowledge of Latin and Greek grammar, and ability to construe the works of classical authors, and some acquaintance with the history of classical times—yet one of the results of education that is most frequently revealed is appreciative acquaintance with the best of English literature of the present and the recent past, and a sound taste and judgement in all aesthetic matters. Marianne Dashwood, lamenting in *Sense and Sensibility* that Edward Ferrars' taste leaves much to be desired, is overstating a case which yet has a real existence:

> 'Music seems scarcely to attract him, and though he admires Elinor's drawings very much, it is not the admiration of a person who can understand their worth. It is evident, in spite of his frequent attention to her while she draws, that in fact he knows nothing of the matter. He admires as a lover, not as a connoisseur.'
>
> (*SS*, 3)

The novels contain professed connoisseurs, like General Tilney in *Northanger Abbey*, with his strictures on bow-windows—'if there is one thing more than another my aversion, it is a patched-on bow' (*NA*, 26)—and also those who, like Mr Knightley, profess nothing at all, who yet can produce, for Mr Woodhouse's entertainment, 'books of engravings, drawers of medals, cameos, corals, shells, and every other family collection within his cabinets' (*E*, 42).

Girls and their education were much less thought of than boys, but are much more important to Jane Austen's novels, where women are observed in much closer detail than men. What makes up a young woman's education is not very clearly defined, for there is no long-established curriculum, like that in the classics for boys. Learning is, however, becoming not only a more desirable, but a more essential, equipment than it was even in the middle of the eighteenth century. Literacy generally is increasing in esteem, that of women along with it. An entertaining literary contrast is noted by Sir Walter Scott, in *Old Mortality*, who, having made a hero out of the historical Marquis of Claverhouse, reproduces in his notes one of his actual letters, on which Scott comments that he 'spelt like a chambermaid'.[1] Scott, Jane Austen's contemporary, demands accurate orthography in a soldier; Henry Tilney, Jane Austen's creation, finds it lacking in young women:

> 'As far as I have had the opportunity of judging, it appears to me that the usual style of letter-writing among women is faultless, except in three particulars.'
> 'And what are they?'
> 'A general deficiency of subject, a total inattention to stops, and a very frequent ignorance of grammar.'
>
> (*NA*, 3)

The remark, though plainly an exaggeration, is a sign of the times; orthodox spelling and regular grammar are now essential equipment, as was far from the case even fifty years before.

The means by which girls get their learning, and what it is, are less clearly laid down. Whereas a quite recent age simply equipped a middle-class girl to be a good head of her household—able to read and write, to keep accounts, to know all the detailed and various business of household management—by the beginning of the nineteenth century something more is generally accepted as desirable. As life becomes easier and more prosperous, with the ordinary home becoming more opulent and comfortable, a young woman becomes free to concentrate on social accomplishments: music, a very desirable art when all entertainment begins at home; arts that are decorative as well as useful, like needlework

---

[1] End note on 'The Skirmish at Drumclog', to *Old Mortality*, Chapter 16.

A square piano.

and painting; and the more fashionable languages, like French and Italian. Such an emphasis can very soon lead to what is superficial and showy, as Jane Austen, along with many of her contemporaries, was quick to expose: she has many instances of women who give up their accomplishments as soon as they have won husbands with them, and she notes that Fanny Price, baronet's niece as she is, is soon despised by the young ladies of Portsmouth, 'for as she neither played on the pianoforte nor wore fine pelisses, they could, on farther observation, admit no right of superiority' (*MP*, 40). Jane Austen reveals that such faulty judgement may co-exist alongside the means of obtaining even a good education. Fanny Price profits from what has produced only complacency in her wealthy cousins Maria and Julia Bertram, as their reactions reveal when they first meet:

'only think, my cousin cannot put the map of Europe together—or my cousin cannot tell the principal rivers in Russia—or she never heard of Asia Minor—or she does not know the difference between water-colours and crayons!—How strange!—Did you ever hear anything so stupid? . . . I am sure I should have been ashamed of myself, if I had not known better long before I was so old as she is. I cannot remember the time when I did not know a great deal that she has not the least notion of yet. How long ago is it, aunt, since we used to repeat the chronological order of the kings of England, with the dates of their accession, and most of the principal events of their reigns?'

'Yes,' added the other; 'and of the Roman Emperors as low as Severus; besides a great deal of Heathen Mythology, and all the Metals, Semi-Metals, Planets, and distinguished philosophers.'

(*MP*, 2)

This ridiculous confusion of misapplied information and vanity reveals how firmly Jane Austen is of her age in holding that education must, even more important than providing knowledge, be a training in character and morals—as it clearly is not for Maria and Julia. Jane Austen recognises the value of accomplishments, both to the possessor and to society: Anne Elliot, in *Persuasion*,

very much preferring the office of musician to a more active post, played country dances to them by the hour together; a kindness which always recommended her musical powers to the notice of Mr and Mrs Musgrove more than anything else, and often drew this compliment,—'Well done Miss Anne! very well done indeed! Lord bless me! how those little fingers of yours fly about!'

The comic point here is that the value of Anne's music is much greater than the social service it provides.

The responsibility for a young woman's education, after the essentials have been supplied, is largely, at this period and in Jane Austen's world and opinion, her own. Examples abound of characters who condemn themselves by failing to fulfil their responsibility. Indeed the two Dashwood sisters, Elinor and Marianne, in *Sense and Sensibility*, are the only ones seen engaging in self-improvement. They fill their days with useful reading, with drawing and painting (Elinor), and music (Marianne) which are clearly too seriously taken to be mere time-filling, or mere escape from other duties and obligations—having a small, rented house on another man's estate, they have no household duties, and few social ones. Most other girls do not do so well, and their fallings-off reveal both the actual and the ideal. The younger Bennet girls in *Pride and Prejudice* waste their time in visits and chatter, except for Mary, who pedantically studies, to no good purpose, 'thorough bass and human nature.' Elizabeth is willing to admit her own deficiencies, and the force of Lady Catherine's just, though grossly impertinent, comments:

> 'My fingers,' said Elizabeth, 'do not move over this instrument in the masterly manner which I see so many women's do. They have not the same force or rapidity, and do not produce the same expression. But then I have always supposed it to be my own fault— because I would not take the trouble of practising. . . .'
>
> 'Miss Bennet would not play at all amiss, if she practised more, and could have the advantage of a London master. She has a very good notion of fingering, though her taste is not equal to Anne's.'
>
> *(PP*, 31)

Emma Woodhouse also stands condemned for not properly attending to her own improvement: though talented, she does not play as well as Jane Fairfax, and does not persevere enough to draw really well. One must give Emma some credit, however, for continuing her self-improvement when, at twenty-one, she is the mistress of her father's house, and undertakes all the duties of a married woman.

The ways by which girls may be taught are various, and all less formal than those for boys. There are no public schools or universities for them. Schooling may be solely the mother's business, as it is Mrs Morland's in *Northanger Abbey*. But the Morlands are not wealthy, and the obvious next cheapest alternative is a school, if it is to be had, such as Jane Austen and her elder sister went to for a short time at Reading, and such as Mrs Goddard's, attended by Emma's pretty friend Harriet Smith, the illegitimate daughter of (as it proves) a prosperous shop-owner. The impression given by Mrs Goddard's school is that the standard is not high, and that this may be not the best way to do things, although, on the other hand, it does not infuse such perniciously false standards as the expensive private education of the Miss Bertrams (instanced above):

> Mrs Goddard was the mistress of a School—not of a seminary, or an establishment, or any thing which professed, in long sentences of refined nonsense, to combine liberal acquirements with elegant

morality upon new principles and new systems—and where young ladies for enormous pay might be screwed out of health and into vanity—but a real, honest, old-fashioned Boarding-school, where a reasonable quantity of accomplishments were sold at a reasonable price, and where girls might be sent to be out of the way and scramble themselves into a little education, without any danger of coming back prodigies. Mrs Goddard's school was in high repute— and very deservedly; for Highbury was reckoned a particularly healthy spot: she had an ample house and garden, gave the children plenty of wholesome food, let them run about a great deal in the summer, and in winter dressed their chilblains with her own hands.

(*E*, 3)

This is plainly not a very high-class place, for higher are suggested by the allusions to 'seminaries' and 'establishments', such as Thackeray recreates in Miss Pinkerton's Academy, with which he opens *Vanity Fair*, which claims to have received a eulogium from the great lexicographer Dr Johnson himself.

The Bennet family in *Pride and Prejudice* enjoyed what may well have been the education of many girls from comfortably-off families, who did not give much serious thought to education, as the inquisitive Lady Catherine, questioning Elizabeth, soon reveals:

'Has your governess left you?'

'We never had any governess.'

'No governess! How was that possible? Five daughters brought up at home without a governess!—I never heard of such a thing. Your mother must have been quite a slave to your education.'

Elizabeth could hardly help smiling, as she assured her that had not been the case.

'Then, who taught you? who attended to you? Without a governess you must have been neglected.'

'Compared with some families, I believe we were; but such of us as wished to learn, never wanted the means. We were always encouraged to read, and had all the masters that were necessary.'

(*PP*, 29)

The obvious solution is the commonest, the one Lady Catherine offers here, the governess. Again Jane Austen suggests, although she does not deal with, most sides of the question. Though the lot of a governess may well be an unfortunate, even a miserable, one, and though many governesses may be inadequate and incompetent; yet even so, the system can at its best be valuable and rewarding for both teacher and taught. One most readily recalls Jane Fairfax in *Emma*, brought up to be almost a sister to the child of wealthy parents, intelligent, talented, and accomplished, but, with no fortune or prospects of her own, doomed almost inevitably to the rôle of governess for her adult livelihood. Jane Austen sees as dreadful, and intends the reader to see, the fate that threatens Jane Fairfax as governess in the family of the ill-bred Mrs Elton's no doubt equally ill-bred friends the Smallridges. Yet in the same novel the author has already shown the happy instance of Isabella's and Emma's own governess (whom nobody but Mr Woodhouse could call '*poor* Miss Taylor'), who has been an excellent teacher to them both, and almost a mother to Emma; whom Emma would gladly have kept as friend and companion for the rest of her life, and loses only when Miss Taylor becomes the wife of the worthy Mr Weston. Lady Catherine de Bourgh in *Pride and Prejudice* may be called in evidence again, with her claims to have happily matched governess to employer:

'It is wonderful how many families I have been the means of supplying in that way. I am always glad to get a young person well placed out. Four nieces of Mrs Jenkinson are most delightfully situated through my means; and it was but the other day, that I recommended another young person, who was merely accidentally mentioned to me, and the family are quite delighted with her.'

(*PP*, 29)

Lady Catherine may be boastful, domineering and objectionable, but we have no reason to doubt her efficiency.

Although Jane Austen concerns herself with the education only of the classes below the aristocracy, and above the level represented by trade in towns, or the tenant farmer in the country—that is, the landed gentry and the professional classes—this is a very large and representative part, probably the majority, of the educated population of her day. Whatever her own education may have been—there is no need to take literally her claim to be 'the most unlearned and uninformed female who ever dared to be an authoress',[1] and she was likely, being a daughter in a highly

---

[1] Letter to James Stanier Clarke, librarian to the Prince Regent, 15 November 1815.

literate family, to be better educated than most—she reveals very precise and powerful opinions on this important matter, as upon so many others, not by overt statements but by what are implicit, in situations and remarks, for the reader who is informed enough to appreciate them.

The historian G. M. Trevelyan, in his *Illustrated English Social History*, laments the growing uselessness of women in the beginning of the nineteenth century:

> As the upper and middle classes grew richer, and as the rural gentry fell more under the influence of town life, it became a point of social pride that the young ladies should be taught by a governess in the schoolroom, and thence pass to the drawing-room, and do at all times as little domestic work as possible.
>
> (Vol. IV, Chapter 1)

This judgement Jane Austen's novels bear out; but his next, that

> The ladies in Jane Austen's novels . . . have little to do but read poetry, retail local gossip and await the attentions of the gentlemen.

is a very disputable statement, as an examination of the rôle actually played by women, and that expected of them, in Jane Austen's novels will reveal. It is true that her women do not have to work, to bring in enough to support the family, on farm, in factory, or in home industry. It can often be the case that, as Elizabeth Bennet says, 'those who chose to be idle certainly might'; nevertheless there is plenty required of them without descending from the drawing-room to the barn, or even to the dairy or the kitchen. One must always be wary of characters' explicit statements on such subjects, for they are hardly ever voicing their author's beliefs; but one important conversation, that between the amiable and easy-going Mr Bingley, his friend the distinguished Mr Darcy, Bingley's sister (who would like to be Mrs Darcy), and Elizabeth Bennet, must be quoted, for the information, but not necessarily the opinions, it contains:

> 'It is amazing to me,' said Bingley, 'how young ladies can have patience to be so very accomplished, as they all are.'
>
> 'All young ladies accomplished! [says Miss Bingley] My dear Charles, what do you mean?'
>
> 'Yes, all of them, I think. They all paint tables, cover skreens,

and net purses. I scarcely know any one who cannot do all this, and I am sure I never heard a young lady spoken of for the first time, without being informed that she was very accomplished.'

'Your list of the common extent of accomplishments,' said Darcy, 'has too much truth. The word is applied to many a woman who deserves it no otherwise than by netting a purse, or covering a skreen. But I am very far from agreeing with you in your estimation of ladies in general. I cannot boast of knowing more than half a dozen, in the whole range of my acquaintance, that are really accomplished.'

'Nor I, I am sure,' said Miss Bingley.

'Then,' observed Elizabeth, 'you must comprehend a great deal in your idea of an accomplished woman.'

'Yes; I do comprehend a great deal in it.'

'Oh! certainly,' replied his faithful assistant, 'no one can be really esteemed accomplished, who does not greatly surpass what is usually met with. A woman must have a thorough knowledge of music, singing, drawing, dancing and the modern languages, to deserve the word; and besides all this, she must possess a certain something in her air and manner of walking, the tone of her voice, her address and expressions, or the word will be but half deserved.'

'All this she must possess,' added Darcy, 'and to all this she must yet add something more substantial, in the improvement of her mind by extensive reading.'

'I am no longer surprised at your knowing *only* six accomplished women. I rather wonder now at your knowing *any*.'

(*PP*, 8)

There is no sign that Jane Austen agrees with Miss Bingley's manifesto (though she may with Mr Darcy's addendum), but such a list shows that even those who live for show and to attract 'the attentions of gentlemen' have plenty to do.

Jane Austen's novels show that life is organised—as civilised life generally is—so that, though it is possible to be idle, there are plenty of things that ought to be done. The novels have their examples of the idle, who are always blameable. The increase in the number of servants allowed a married woman, with a house-keeper to supervise her domestic arrangements, and nursemaids and governesses to take charge of her maternal ones, to be like Lady Bertram of *Mansfield Park*, indolent and sofa-ridden, doing nothing but wool-work and playing cards. It allows unmarried ones to spend their time like the younger Miss Bennets in *Pride and Prejudice*, gossiping, walking to the shops, trimming their dresses and bonnets, and flirting with the militia. Suggestions of idleness are always suggestions of inadequacy, even when more obliquely made:

> Mrs Grant having by this time run through the usual resources of ladies residing in the country without a family of children; having more than filled her favourite sitting-room with pretty furniture, and made a choice collection of plants and poultry, was very much in want of some variety at home.
>
> (*MP*, 4)

Jane Austen plainly does not think this the proper way, and proves it, not only by the examples she gives of usefully occupied women but by the very exposure of defaulters: Mrs Charlotte Palmer in *Sense and Sensibility*, empty-headed, laughing and chattering, goes through merely the motions of proper housewifery when she returns from London to her own house at Cleveland in Somerset:

> the rest of the morning was easily whiled away, in lounging round the kitchen garden, examining the bloom upon its walls, and listening to the gardener's lamentations upon blights,—in dawdling through the green-house, where the loss of her favourite plants, unwarily exposed, and nipped by the lingering frost, raised the laughter of Charlotte,—and in visiting the poultry-yard, where, in the disappointed hopes of her dairy-maid, by hens forsaking their nests, or being stolen by a fox, or in the rapid decrease of a promising brood, she found fresh sources of merriment.
>
> (*SS*, 41)

Women's duties as seen by Jane Austen are essentially what anyone's duties have always been: duties within one's own home, duties to one's neighbours and to society, and the obligation to improve oneself. The proliferation of servants can make the burden of the first lighter for a married woman, and can remove it entirely for an unmarried one; circumstances can only occasionally relieve the second; nothing can remove the third except her own negligence.

Within the home, the woman is the housewife and mother, and where the housekeeping and the upbringing are not done in person she has the full responsibility nevertheless, and becomes, with the larger household, an administrator. Generally speaking, the house and what goes on inside it is the woman's concern, while the estate and what goes on outside are the man's. The exceptions are those mentioned in Mrs Palmer's morning tour above, the flower garden complete, and the shrubbery for recreation and walks. The income from the poultry is traditionally the wife's, and provides 'pin-money', or personal spending money. It is well to recognise these duties and their performance in order to assess characters. Mrs Bennet of *Pride and Prejudice*, nervous and silly as she is, is yet an efficient (though not an economical) housekeeper, with an intelligent and practical interest in her catering; she laments that her husband has invited a guest to dinner when 'there is not a bit of fish to be got today' (*PP*, 13) and congratulates herself after another, more successful occasion, that

> 'The dinner was as well dressed as any I ever saw. The venison was roasted to a turn—and everybody said, they never saw so fat a haunch. The soup was fifty times better than what we had at the Lucases last week; and even Mr Darcy acknowledged, that the partridges were remarkably well done.'
>
> (*PP*, 54)

Servants do not solve all a housewife's problems, as that other silly family, the Prices, demonstrate, those feckless parents whom Fanny Price revisits in *Mansfield Park*. They are not rich, but they are not grimly poor either; their discomfort is plainly caused by the mismanagement of Mrs Price, who, though she has two servants, laments having to do most of the work herself, and lets the upper servant, Rebecca, answer her back. Jane Austen summarises Mrs Price as 'dissatisfied with her servants, without skill to make them better, and whether helping, or reprimanding, or indulging them, without any power of gaining their respect' (*MP*, 39).

The commonest indoor occupation for all women is needlework, not only for pleasure, but as a sober necessity, when everything must be sewn by hand, and mended many times before being deemed fit to be replaced. Wealthy families can hire girls for plain sewing and mending, and indulge themselves with finer work and embroidery. There are many details of needlework in Jane Austen's letters; the reason there are few in the novels is that mere

Jane Austen's 'huswif', containing needlework equipment.

filling-in of familiar background, as this would be, is never her purpose. But the quantity of time plain sewing necessarily consumes (with the sewing-machine half a century ahead) is vividly revealed when Fanny Price, with a brother about to join the navy in under a week, 'set about working for Sam immediately, and by working early and late, with perseverance and great dispatch, did so much, that the boy was shipped off at last, with more than half his linen ready' (*MP*, 39).

In household affairs, one gains from Jane Austen a very pleasant impression of partnership between man and woman, and very little of the dominant *pater familias*. Admittedly the partnership is often between very imperfect beings, but one feels no improbability in Emma ruling both the household of Hartfield and her hypochondriac father. But preconceived notions of the dominant position of men are shaken by the way Sir Walter Elliot in

Persuasion, one of the vainest and most self-satisfied, finding himself overcome with debts, consults not only his daughter Elizabeth but his friend and neighbour Lady Russell.

All women have their duties to society. Charity, since the nineteenth-century over-use of the term and abuse of the concept, has come to have an unpleasant ring, suggesting degrading dependence on capricious and complacent patronage. The reader of Jane Austen must disabuse himself of such notions, and realise that in a society where there is no state aid for the ill, the old, and the out of work, except the work-house and very limited outside relief, the assistance of the distress of others was the moral duty of the prosperous man towards those who depended on him, and receiving it was both necessary and proper. The giving and receiving is a personal matter in small communities, and naturally devolves upon women, who are those most suited by upbringing and training. Again the letters demonstrate that they formed an important part of the author's own life, in the details they contain of visits paid to retired servants, and old people of the parish. In the novels, the small details of concern for the community are always signs of merit. The most benevolent heroine is also the one many readers have found most charming—Anne Elliot in *Persuasion*—through whom severe judgement is passed on her father, Sir Walter, and sister, Elizabeth: Anne alone, when the family leaves Kellynch, undertakes 'going to almost every house in the parish, as a sort of take-leave. I was told they wished it' (*P*, 5). When at Bath, she has no hesitations about visiting her former school-friend, now an impecunious invalid, living shabbily and unfashionably. Anne is only a private person; Lady Catherine de Bourgh, in *Pride and Prejudice*, suggests both the duties of a lady of the manor, and the proper performance of them, by her own comic limitations:

> though this lady was not in the commission of the peace for the country, she was the most active magistrate in her own parish ... and whenever any of the cottagers were disposed to be quarrelsome, discontented or too poor, she sallied forth into the village to settle their differences, silence their complaints, and scold them into harmony and plenty.
>
> (*PP*, 30)

Critics have noted Emma Woodhouse's remarks on the condition of the poor, and deduced from them that she is frivolous; there can be little doubt that the contrary is intended, and that the words are sound unsentimental sense:

> 'If we feel for the wretched, enough to do all we can for them, the rest is empty sympathy, only distressing to ourselves.'

$$(E, 10)$$

The last category of duties, self-improvement, is the one that can cause the most misunderstanding, since many of the occupations comprehended in it can all too easily be dismissed as idling—notably drawing and painting, fine needlework, and, above all, reading. These are the most obvious occupations of the young, unmarried woman, who, since she usually has no household cares, has the most time available for them. The heroines who appear to take their duty of self-improvement most seriously are Elinor and Marianne Dashwood in *Sense and Sensibility*. Living in a small, rented cottage, they can have few other obligations, and devote themselves to what is really self-education, along the lines on which they have most talent, Elinor in drawing, Marianne in music. Jane Austen herself is not musical, so beyond the odd mention of Italian songs or Scotch airs, there is no reflection of contemporary taste, or hint that this is the age when Beethoven and Schubert are writing, and Mozart in vogue. Nor is she particularly artistic, giving no allusions to painters in her novels, even though she shows herself better informed and interested in her letters, which tell of visits to London exhibitions.

With drawing, painting, and needlework, social and personal benefits overlap. The uses of sewing are obvious and have been mentioned. A musician is a valuable asset when entertainment in the country, even for the prosperous, had to be self-made or done without. The musician may be the entertainer herself, like Emma and Jane Fairfax at the Coles's dinner-party, or the supplier of entertainment, like Anne Elliot playing country-dances at Uppercross.

Reading is a very comprehensive word, and entails efforts more strenuous than those expended on novels and the newspapers. It is closer in sense to that still surviving in the expression 'reading for a degree'. Marianne Dashwood is ridiculed for her excesses, but reads many serious and valuable things. She reads poetry—

Thomson, Cowper and Scott—and 'would have every book that tells her how to admire an old twisted tree'; anyone who has read Gilpin on the Picturesque, or its like (to which the jibe refers) knows that they are serious studies in taste, and not to be read lightly. Recovering from her illness, she proposes an impossible programme:

> 'I have formed my plan, and am determined to enter on a course of serious study. . . . By reading only six hours a-day, I shall gain in the course of a twelvemonth a great deal of instruction which I now feel myself to want.'
>
> Elinor honoured her for a plan which originated so nobly as this; though smiling to see the same eager fancy which had been leading her to the extreme of languid indolence and selfish repining, now at work in introducing excess into a scheme of such rational employment and virtuous self-control.
>
> (*SS*, 45)

The sensible Elinor shows us exactly how such a use of time is to be judged. Even Emma, who with a household to govern might be thought excused from further self-education, knows she should attend to it, and is wryly rebuked by Mr Knightley for not doing so. Minor characters who neglect self-improvement are self-condemned: Lady Middleton, for instance, in *Sense and Sensibility* 'had celebrated [her marriage] by giving up music, although by her mother's account she had played extremely well, and by her own was very fond of it' (*SS*, 8).

While the opportunities for a full and satisfying life within the accepted domestic framework of things are greater than they look at first, it is of course much more obvious that outside it the prospect for the unprovided woman is grim. Jane Fairfax braces herself for what she well knows will probably be a hard life as a governess, proving that Jane Austen knows that most governesses are not so lucky as Emma's own Miss Taylor, in finding a prosperous, cheerful Mr Weston to marry them. Mrs Elton's résumé of what the accomplished governess can demand merely makes one shudder at the lot of the young woman who cannot offer such talents:

> 'Your musical knowledge alone would entitle you to name your own terms, have as many rooms as you like, and mix in the family

as much as you chose;—that is—I do not know—if you knew the
harp, you might do all that, I am very sure; but you sing as well as
play;—yes, I really believe you might, even without the harp,
stipulate for what you chose.'

(*E*, 35)

one agrees with Jane that employment agencies are 'offices for the
sale—not quite of human flesh—but of human intellect' (*ibid.*).

It should be equally clear that the future is dark for Miss Bates, a
middle-aged spinster with a very small income, no profession, and
no-one but her mother; and not bright even for the young, and
pretty, and stupid Harriet Smith, who has no hope but to marry
comfortably. In fact, the last word on the subject is the cool-
headed Charlotte Lucas's (whom it is easy to judge too harshly
for marrying Mr Collins, 'neither sensible nor agreeable') that
marriage is 'the only honourable provision for well-educated
young women of small fortune, and however uncertain of giving
happiness, must be their pleasantest preservative from want'
(*PP*, 22). When this resource fails, there is little left, as witnessed
by the unfortunate widow Mrs Smith in *Persuasion*, living in two
rooms in Bath, crippled by rheumatism, unable to act for herself
to improve the confused affairs left by her husband, able only to
knit, and that not to bring in money for herself, but for charitable
acts to others.

The path of virtue is the best path, not only morally but practically, in Jane Austen's world. Her own morals and those of her
novels are strict, but can be overstated. She is no prude, and has
'no reluctance, no horror, no feminine—shall I say? no modest
loathings' (such as Edmund Bertram would, very oddly, have
liked in Mary Crawford). She has as firm a grip on the situation of
the 'fallen woman' as of the governess. She is closer to the eighteenth
century out of which she comes than the nineteenth which she
enters—that eighteenth century in which the prosperous and even
socially acceptable kept mistress had played a considerable part in
public life; in which sexual lapses were not irretrievable, even in
classes below the aristocracy. Jane Austen's own themes do not
make it often relevant for her to deal with sexual relations between
men and women, outside of courtship and marriage, but like many
other topics, she is aware of their existence, and expects her reader

to be so. Her letters—where she does not create or select her material but takes what life offers her for the amusement of her correspondents, and has no artistic or moral purpose in view—are very much more robustly outspoken than her novels.

Within the novels, only one girl lives with a man unmarried, and only one wife commits adultery. The foolish Lydia Bennet (who runs off with Wickham from Brighton), her situation, and probable eventual fate, are an indirect condemnation of the growing strictness of society's code, which could drive the girl, once seduced, into the increasing trade in prostitution. The characters who desire the conventional fate for Lydia are the least estimable ones, and Jane Austen derives a good deal of astringent humour from them. The neighbourhood of the Bennets reacts thus to hearing that Lydia is married:

> To be sure it would have been more for the advantage of conversation, had Miss Lydia Bennet come upon the town; or, as the happiest alternative, been secluded from the world, in some distant farm house.
>
> *(PP*, 50)

while Mr Collins in his joint capacity as cleric and cousin, exhorts Mr Bennet in a letter:

> Let me advise you then, my dear Sir, to console yourself as much as possible, to throw off your unworthy child from your affection for ever, and leave her to reap the fruits of her own heinous offence.
>
> *(PP*, 48)

Even their marriage does not soften him: he is shocked that Lydia has visited her parents:

> You ought certainly to forgive them as a christian, but never to admit them in your sight, or allow their names to be mentioned in your hearing.
>
> *(PP*, 57)

Maria Bertram in *Mansfield Park*, far more intelligent and self-aware than Lydia, who, having irresponsibly married the vacuous Mr Rushworth for money, irresponsibly elopes with Henry Crawford for love, gets, and deserves, a harsher fate. She actually is secluded in the equivalent of the distant farmhouse that was anticipated for Lydia. Here it is the inestimable character

Mrs Norris who wishes to defend Maria, and the estimable father who is inflexible:

> Maria had destroyed her own reputation, and he would not by a vain attempt to restore what never could be restored, be affording his sanction to vice, or in seeking to lessen its disgrace, be anywise accessary to introducing such misery in another man's family, as he had known himself.
>
> (*MP*, 48)

Jane Austen condemns the irresponsibility and the harm to others rather than the act. Maria, being clever, married, and deliberately unprincipled both in marrying and in eloping, is a much graver offender than the young and empty-headed Lydia.

Jane Austen never suggests that society as a whole is as well-regulated as that in her novels. She assumes that we know it is not, and only says so where necessary. The unsatisfactory Admiral Crawford, of whom we hear in *Mansfield Park*, who has had the upbringing of his niece and nephew, Mary and Henry Crawford, keeps a mistress; the extravagant and irresponsible Willoughby in *Sense and Sensibility* has seduced and deserted Colonel Brandon's ward Eliza; we hear of these two only because their acts outside the story affect the action within it. Otherwise Jane Austen, knowledgeable as her reader, is content to remain silent and, as she says 'let other pens dwell on guilt and misery' (*MP*, 48).

In Jane Austen's calm and prosperous country settings it is easy to have the erroneous feeling that men, as well as women, have very little, if anything, to do. Again Jane Austen depends on her reader's knowledge of what life is like, and depends on him to respond to her unobtrusive hints.

Quite clearly some of her male characters *do* do very little. Some do it in their own homes, like Mr Bennet in *Pride and Prejudice*, who can sit in his library reading for the whole of what she terms the morning (that is, until dinner-time in the late afternoon); some waste their time like Tom Bertram, on sport, shooting, hunting, and horse-racing. A number of the men in the novels are seen when on visits—like Mr Darcy, in *Pride and Prejudice*, or Mr Crawford, in *Mansfield Park*—and seem to have nothing to prevent these visits being long ones. A casual modern reader might suppose from what is obviously before him that men, having breakfasted, amuse themselves, generally out of doors, until it is time for dinner, when they rejoin the ladies for food and entertainment until bed-time.

As the evening and dinner are the times at which men and women meet these are clearly the times on which Jane Austen's novels dwell most fully. But equally clearly those men with professions have the duties that pertain to them, which will be dealt with in due course. But Jane Austen's men must first be divided on another system. They are of two sorts: those who are rich and idle enough to consider the country as habitable only for sport—for shooting and fishing, and the recently introduced fox-hunting—who live in town, generally London, for the 'season'; and those who, though they may hunt, shoot, and fish, and may visit London or other resorts, really live and have their home in the country. The latter is the commoner and larger group, and is probably the more representative of the passing eighteenth century, while the former presages the advancing nineteenth century. The distinction is not one of class, but of *mores* and temperament; in Jane Austen, particularly in *Mansfield Park*, it becomes almost a moral distinction, with her approval bestowed upon the old ways.

Most of Jane Austen's men own land, in estates both modest and wealthy, comprising either a large area, farmed both by squire and by tenant farmers, like Mr Knightley's Donwell in *Emma*, or Sir Thomas Bertram's Mansfield, or a very much smaller estate like Mr Bennet's in *Pride and Prejudice*, which has a 'manor' on which he shoots, but is apparently no more than he can farm himself. Such men are necessarily landlords, or farmers, or both. Jane Austen does not detail their activities—we should never discover, if Jane Bennet did not want the horses to visit her friends the Bingleys, that Mr Bennet had a farm on which they were needed—but she notes sharply what happens when they do not perform them. Sir Walter Elliot in *Persuasion* is vain, improvident, and foolish; he has, despite an able deputy in his agent Mr Shepherd, overspent his income from his Kellynch estates, mortgaged all of them that he can, and is finally forced to let his house and live modestly in Bath. Henry Crawford in *Mansfield Park* should excite disapproval for being an absentee landlord of his estate in Somerset, who goes there only for the opening of the shooting season. When he attempts to ingratiate himself with

Harleston Park, Northamptonshire, supposedly the original of Mansfield Park.

Fanny Price, talks to her of his plans for improving it, and his suspicion that his agent there is not doing his job honestly, the acute reader registers the more forcibly how long he has been neglecting his duties. Jane Austen does not involve herself or her reader in any more elaborate detail, but she is plainly as well aware of the harm done by an irresponsible landlord as is her contemporary, Maria Edgeworth. Miss Edgeworth felt one of her duties in writing was to expose the derelictions of such landlords in Ireland, and does so in a number of her stories—*Castle Rackrent* and *The Absentee*, written in 1800 and 1801, are probably the best known—by humorous and ironic exposure often very like Jane Austen's own. Jane Austen can rely upon her reader's knowing the English variety so well in real life that it would be superfluous to write of it as Miss Edgeworth does, just as she can rely upon readers' having met examples of the model proprietor also, like Fielding's Squire Allworthy in *Tom Jones*. She does not therefore dwell upon the ways in which Sir Thomas Bertram governs his Northamptonshire estates, even though it is very clear that he is most conscientious and efficient in managing them. When he returns from his long absence in Antigua she merely mentions that

> It was a busy morning with him. Conversation with any of them occupied but a small part of it. He had to reinstate himself in all the wonted concerns of his Mansfield life, to see his steward and bailiff —to examine and compute—and in the intervals of business, to walk into his stables and his gardens, and nearest plantations; but active and methodical, he had . . . done all this before he resumed his seat as master of the house at dinner.
>
> (*MP*, 20)

Plainly the absence of fuss is part of the efficiency, and another proof that Sir Thomas is a man who takes his duties seriously, and does them as thoroughly at home as he has done those in the estates in Antigua which have caused him to be so long away. The reader who does not feel and acknowledge Sir Thomas's social and public worth (he is an M.P.) is likely to judge him too harshly for his failures in personal relationships, in the upbringing of his daughters, and in understanding his niece Fanny Price, in particular when he is angry with her for refusing to marry Henry Crawford. But all the evidence is offered. The only man with whom the modern reader might be misled is Mr Darcy in *Pride and Prejudice*, who, during most of the novel, is away from home, visiting his friend Bingley at Netherfield, staying in London, or with his aunt, Lady Catherine, at Rosings. Jane Austen to some degree intends to mislead the reader because the heroine Elizabeth Bennet is misled herself. He is presented, first, simply as a man worth ten thousand a year; the estate in Derbyshire is mentioned and viewed only as the source of so desirable an income. But when Elizabeth begins to realise that she has misjudged him, and to adopt a fairer view of him, Jane Austen allows the reader, with Elizabeth, to see more of him. Darcy becomes more attractive, and one of the chief ways in which Jane Austen creates his attraction is by presenting him at home in his own house and on his own lands at Pemberley in Derbyshire. He becomes the young lord of the manor who has the unstinted praise of the housekeeper, who has made his house attractive without ostentation, and its grounds picturesque:

> 'He is the best landlord, and the best master,' said she, 'that ever lived. Not like the wild young men now-a-days, who think of

nothing but themselves. There is not one of his tenants or servants but what will give him a good name.'

(PP, 43)

In such terms he appears to Elizabeth in her newly softened mood towards him. One of the first qualities to make him seem a possible husband is that he is a perfect landlord.

The landlord's obligations are clearly great: to his tenants, to his lands (this is the great era of agricultural improvement), to his own household, and as the patron of the church, arts, and learning. All these are frequently touched upon or suggested, and at all times implicitly understood. Those who fail, frequently point out the quality they lack. Two of the most outrageously memorable are Mr John Dashwood, and his wife, who, while persuading him into doing nothing to help his widowed step-mother and half-sisters (the heroines of *Sense and Sensibility*) exposes the failings of another:

'my mother was clogged with the payment of three (annuities) to old superannuated servants by my father's will, and it is amazing how disagreeable she found it. . . . Her income was not her own, she said, with such perpetual claims on it; and it was the more unkind in my father, because, otherwise, the money would have been entirely at my mother's disposal, without any restriction whatever.'

(SS, 2)

A whole layer of obligations is suggested by Mrs Elton in *Emma*, boasting of her husband the vicar's commitments:

'He really is engaged from morning to night.—There is no end of people's coming to him, on some pretence or other.—The magistrates, and overseers, and church wardens, are always wanting his opinion. They seem not to be able to do anything without him.'

(E, 52)

No mere vicar is so indispensable, but what she says would be true of Mr Knightley, of whom Emma herself, delighted to have him confirm that Harriet Smith will marry Robert Martin, suggests a host of other concerns:

'Did not you misunderstand him?—You were both talking of other things; of business, shows of cattle, or new drills—and might not you, in the confusion of so many subjects, mistake him?—It was

A gentleman's library at Iveagh House, Kenwood.

not Harriet's hand that he was certain of—it was the dimensions of some famous ox.'

(E, 54)

Only from such slight hints do we realise that Jane Austen is writing of the age of Coke of Norfolk who, introducing new crops and new methods, so improved his estates at Holkham that between 1776–1816 he raised their annual rental from £2,200 to £20,000; and that almost as close are 'Turnip' Townshend (whose nickname is self-explanatory) and Robert Bakewell of Leicestershire, who concentrated on improving the breed of sheep and cattle.

Finally, there is the obligation to be, if not a connoisseur, at least a man of taste. This is the great age not only of the country house and of landscape gardening but also of perhaps the finest productions of English craftsmen, in everything pertaining to the inside of the house, to decoration, to furniture, and the general contents. Prosperity produces the demand for more, and finer, things, and the supply of them fortunately produced a high standard. Intelligent and well-informed patronage caused all arts to flourish. Mr Darcy sees it as his duty to enlarge the library he has inherited:

'What a delightful library you have at Pemberley, Mr Darcy!'

'It ought to be good,' he replied, 'it has been the work of many generations.'

'And then you have added to it so much yourself, you are always buying books.'

'I cannot comprehend the neglect of a library in such days as these.'

(PP, 8)

General Tilney of Northanger Abbey is the great patron in the novels; his motive is very plainly pride and ostentation which, however deplorable, causes him to patronise the best of the modern useful arts in a way that is common among actual persons of the period. Jane Austen causes her reader to question the motives behind his taste, but never the taste itself. He has admirably modernised his medieval house (though in a way that Catherine Morland, full of the Gothic and the romantic, deplores), attending both to harmony and to comfort, and equipped it with furnishings

A tea service in Worcester china.

chosen with conscious assurance. Again Jane Austen confines herself to details, to suggest the whole, such as the Staffordshire breakfast set, whose elegance attracts Catherine's notice. The general's disclaimer that 'for his part, to his uncritical palate, the tea was as well flavoured from the clay of Staffordshire, as from that of Dresden or Sêve [sic]' (*NA*, 22) is merely an inverted boast, for this is the hey-day of the English china manufacturers, who, setting themselves in the later eighteenth century to rival Sèvres and Meissen, rapidly did so with their equally famous works at Chelsea, Bow, Derby, and Worcester. The general may even be referring to Josiah Wedgwood's factory at Barlaston, which devoted itself to popular and cheaper versions, whose quality and design is no less excellent.

A Wedgwood plate, from a service made for the Prince Regent.

CHAPTER FOUR

Getting and Spending

ALTHOUGH Jane Austen is sometimes accused of being mercenary and of allowing money to take too large a share of her heroine's calculations, she yet seems to spend little time on the actual earning of money. As the previous chapter has shown, women have few opportunities to do so, and, if they are fortunate, do not need them; while the men who are fortunate enough to belong to the landed gentry have enough to live prosperously, so that their task is to make the best use of the goods they are born with or inherit.

Not all men of the middle class, or even of the gentry themselves, are so fortunate. An estate can usually be inherited only by the eldest son. Many are entailed upon the nearest male relative, as Mr Bennet's is in *Pride and Prejudice* upon his cousin Mr Collins. He cannot leave any of it to his daughters and, as Mrs Bennet so melodramatically puts it, 'the Collinses will turn us all out, before he is cold in his grave' (*PP*, 47). Even where there is apparently no entail, as in *Mansfield Park*, there seems to be no thought of dividing the estate: the eldest son Tom Bertram will inherit, and Edmund must be supported by entering the church, so that he can be given the Mansfield and Thornton Lacey parishes as a living. Younger sons of noblemen, landowners, and gentry must find professions for themselves, or have them obtained for them. Although Edward Ferrars in *Sense and Sensibility* is an elder son, he summarises the situation very clearly, in his ironical bitterness at being helplessly dependent on his capricious mother:

'It has been, and is, and probably will always be a heavy misfortune to me, that I have had no necessary business to engage me, no profession to give me employment, or afford me any thing like independence. But unfortunately my own nicety, and the nicety of my friends, have made me what I am, an idle, helpless being. We never could agree in our choice of profession. I always preferred the church, and still do. But that was not smart enough for my family. They recommended the army. That was a great deal too smart for me. The law was allowed to be genteel enough; many young men, who had chambers in the Temple, made a very good appearance in the first circles, and drove about town in very knowing gigs. But I had no inclination for the law, even in this less abstruse study of it, which my family approved. As for the navy, it had fashion on its side, but I was too old when the subject was first started to enter it—and, at length, as there was no necessity for my having any profession at all, as I might be as dashing and expensive without a red coat on my back as with one, idleness was pronounced on the whole to be the most advantageous and honourable.'

(*SS*, 19)

The openings he sees for himself are what many young men in his position saw, and what were all that offered to most younger sons. Trade of any sort is clearly not a natural or proper calling for a gentleman—indeed it is part of the social shame of the Bennet family, in the snobbish Lady Catherine's eyes, that they have an uncle in trade; and the aim of most of the men in business who appear in the novels has been to make enough money to retire from it and live as country gentlemen, like Mr Weston and the Coles in *Emma*.

Although the order of fashion places the army, navy, and law higher than the Church as desirable ways for a man to support himself, Jane Austen gives us fewer soldiers than lawyers, fewer of either than sailors, and fewer sailors even than clergymen. A rector's daughter, and sister to both rectors and sailors, she plainly felt herself both familiar and competent when creating them in her novels. Moreover, they suit her purposes and subject-matter well, in belonging to professions that keep men at home and in domestic life for long periods.

There are few soldiers in Jane Austen's novels, and of those all are of the commissioned ranks, and few details are given of their military duties either in peace or war. Before the Napoleonic War, the army was generally speaking unpopular with people in general because it only came to their notice when being employed as a police force in times of public unrest, to quell rioting, or root out

Left A corporal, and *right* a commander from the South Gloucester Militia.

smuggling. As Trevelyan[1] remarks, 'It is a wonder that our ancestors preserved public order and private property as well as they did'. The army became, however, popular and esteemed as soon as it had a purpose, especially during the Peninsular War of 1808–14. Jane Austen's is a period of changes in the army, caused by these long campaigns against Napoleon. A standing army is now accepted as a necessary institution, and supplants the militia as the country's defence against invasion. The militia now come to be a body from whom regular soldiers may be recruited, like Wickham in *Pride and Prejudice* who, when finally induced to marry Lydia, leaves the Hertfordshire militia for the regular army and a station in Newcastle. After Waterloo, a small army only is maintained; it is likely that Jane Austen, remarking of Wickham and Lydia that the peace 'dismissed them to a home', is anticipating the peace that had not yet been agreed at the time of which she purports to be writing.[2] A novelist is under no obligation to

[1] *Illustrated English Social History*, III, Chapter 2.
[2] She used almanacks of the years 1811 and 1812 to plan the dates and events of the story.

Left A Field Officer and Private of the Royal Engineers, and *right* an Officer of the 9th Light Dragoons.

follow history, and may quite properly, in recounting the future of her characters, anticipate the future of their world and her own.

In the army even more than the navy there is an almost impassable gulf between the ranks—which even Wellington called 'the scum of the earth'—and the officers. Although Jane Austen feels no call to dwell upon the degrading conditions suffered by the common soldier, she shows herself as aware as her contemporaries of the brutal discipline enforced. Such facts as that one soldier in the time of George II received 30,000 lashes in sixteen years must be brought to mind when she remarks in passing, as part of the Meryton gossip, that 'a private had been flogged'. Plainly, Meryton is not callous enough to take such things in its stride—neither is Jane Austen.

Being the most fashionable profession, the army draws from the aristocracy as well as the gentry, and is thus an appropriately flashy calling for that self-seeking rogue Wickham. It was easy for army officers to have very little to do with their men, leaving their care and control to the sergeants, and leaving themselves free to idle, trifle, flirt, and waste their time and money, as do, apparently, the militia stationed at Meryton. Another reason why the army is aristocratic is that in the first instances it costs money rather than provides it. Every rank has to be bought, at prices ranging from £400 for an ensigncy to £2,600 for a majority; for which advertisements appeared regularly in newspapers. It was cheaper to join the militia; an ensigncy in 1803 cost only £10—probably the original reason why Wickham joined it rather than the regulars.

Though the army increased rapidly in size and importance during the period when Jane Austen was writing—from between 80,000 and 90,000 in 1800, to 105,000 in 1810—the only novel on which the army seriously impinges is *Pride and Prejudice*. Although a colonel (Brandon) appears in *Sense and Sensibility*, his rank merely attests a worthy, and middle-aged, character, while Captain Tilney in *Northanger Abbey* is merely characterised as following the most fashionable calling for an eldest son. The militia overrun Meryton in *Pride and Prejudice*, or at least, the officers do, not only metaphorically, because all the silly young women's heads are turned by them and their red coats, but literally, because at this time there were no barracks for them, and they were all forced to find lodgings for themselves.

The navy might well be thought to have less part in the life of rural gentry than the army, since its activities necessarily happen not at home but at sea. But Jane Austen, who had two brothers who became admirals, and who lived for some time at Portsmouth, finds it easy and natural to use facts about ships, and sailors, especially in her later novels *Mansfield Park* and *Persuasion*. But even here she assumes much more knowledge than she imparts. One would not guess from her work that this is one of the navy's finest eras, with its victories over the French, under Nelson; nor that this is the inglorious age of the press-gang, of brutal ill-treatment, of disgusting conditions, and occasionally of mutiny. It is easy to overstate both the glory and the degradation: Jane Austen did neither; knowing both, she chose not to use them. The press-gang was the terror of coastal districts, where merchant sailors or mere ordinary able-bodied landsmen could be seized from the quaysides, from ale-houses, or even from convivial gatherings like weddings, to serve on ships and follow a way of life

Left A Lieutenant, and *right* a Captain of the Royal Navy.

too uncongenial to attract volunteers. Mrs Gaskell, writing nearly fifty years later, recalls in *Sylvia's Lovers* the way press-gangs seized men who were freshly back in Whitby after months spent whale-hunting in the Arctic, while Thomas Hardy treats the perils of the merchant seaman ashore more humorously in *The Trumpet-Major*.

On board ship, life was inevitably rough and, cut off as it necessarily was from all but itself, depended on the quality of the captain and his officers whether it was made tolerable. In an age when punishments in general were so vicious and life so hard, it is easy to overstate the individual case. But among the ratings the company was uncouth, the quarters necessarily cramped, and the food and pay inadequate, with alcoholic liquor one of the few compensations for all else. There is no need to stress the discomforts of a way of life in which men often contracted scurvy from mal-nutrition, where the main food was salt pork and beef (nicknamed 'old horse'), and ship's biscuit made of inferior corn and likely to

H.M. Frigate *Triton*, by Nicholas Pocock.

degenerate into the 'biscuit-worms' fed to the albatross according to the early version of Coleridge's poem *The Ancient Mariner*.

Jane Austen is quite as concerned to remove other misapprehensions, those of girls who suppose 'sailors to be living on board without anything to eat, or any cook to dress it if there were, or any servant to wait, or any knife and fork to use' (*P*, 8). Mrs Croft, an admiral's wife, can say 'women may be as comfortable on board, as in the best house in England' and 'nothing can exceed the accommodations of a man of war; I speak, you know of the higher rates. When you come to a frigate, of course, you are more confined—though any reasonable woman may be perfectly happy in one of them' (*P*, 8).

The navy enjoyed a high reputation and, like the almost equally ill-treated army, behaved itself magnificently in its various engagements. This was partly the result of the type and general standard of its officers. They were generally of more modest origins than the army's, the sons (like Nelson himself) of gentlemen who could not afford to launch them in other professions, who went to sea as boys, at the rank of midshipman, and worked their way up gradually, partly by influence and patronage, but also by merit. In the navy as in other professions, however, patronage and purchase are accepted ways to advancement. In *Mansfield Park*, Fanny's brother William Price the midshipman despairs of becoming a lieutenant on his own merit before he is so old as to lose all joy in the promotion—and having become one, he has then to aspire to the next step:

> what can be more unbecoming, or more worthless, than the uniform of a lieutenant, who has been a lieutenant a year or two, and sees others made commanders before him?

(MP, 37)

His delight has no sense of guilt when Henry Crawford gets him his promotion, using his uncle the admiral, who in turn uses a friend, who in turn uses a Secretary to the First Lord of the Admiralty.

The great merit of the navy still remains, that it is a profession in which one can rise by personal effort, particularly if the effort is assisted by a war. Captain Wentworth in *Persuasion* has done so, despite the humble and uncertain beginnings which caused Anne to break off her engagement to him. Made a commander in consequence of the action of St Domingo, he has to wait for a ship to be appointed to him, and to depend for wealth upon prize money obtained by capturing enemy vessels. But he can fairly say:

> 'I have been used to the gratification of believing myself to earn every blessing that I enjoyed.'

(P, 21)

Equally his young friend Captain Benwick can be commiserated for being 'only a commander, it is true, made last summer, and these are bad times for getting on' (*P*, 18)—meaning that there is at present peace at sea. Whereas prize money may be considerable —one ship was awarded £200,000 in 1805 for capturing some Spanish frigates—pay was not: the *Morning Post* for 9 October 1801 states that 'Post Captains in the Navy are to have 8/– a day instead of six. And it is supposed that Lieutenants will be advanced to four shillings instead of three.'[1]

There are many clergymen among Jane Austen's characters. The rector or vicar, next to the landowner, occupied the most influential place in rural life, and was frequently a relation. Jane Austen always assumes the importance of the clerical office, though she is happy to delineate faulty holders of it. Modern

---

[1] From *The Dawn of the XIXth Century in England*, John Ashton, Fisher Unwin, 1906.

'The Reverend Robert Walker', by Henry Raeburn.

readers, not sharing either her context or her principles, have been uneasy both when she holds up her parsons to ridicule—because through them she seems to be ridiculing religion—and also when she is clearly delineating an estimable cleric, like Edmund Bertram—because in him she seems either to hold very inadequate views of what a clergyman should be and do, or to have created a prig. As so often, Jane Austen points out right standards by fallings-off from them, and assumes a familiarity and agreement on principles which the modern reader does not necessarily possess. Probably more is taken for granted about the clerical office than about any other topic Jane Austen employs; partly because the clergyman's life and duties are what she herself lived with, and were second nature to her, partly because the eighteenth century in the Church of England (which is all that she need concern herself with in novels of rural society) is a time of conformity, when the established Church was not yet split, self-conscious, and defensive, as it later became.

Jane Austen's clerics, like herself and a great proportion of the eighteenth century which bred them, advocate practical and personal benevolence, rather than doctrine or proselytising. Morality must result in public acts, but it must also be a matter for the individual. To be a clergyman is not so much to follow a vocation as to have a job to do, where the onus is on the individual to do it well. The stress is therefore not on forms of worship, or doctrine, but on the whole conduct of life with other men. Her handling of clergymen in the novels becomes gradually more serious. The young Jane Austen makes little in *Northanger Abbey* of Henry Tilney's duties: he may enjoy himself for weeks in Bath, and live at Northanger rather than in his parish at Woodston— although he does say 'Northanger is not more than half my home' (*NA*, 20). Mr Collins in *Pride and Prejudice* is very straightforward comedy, with his grotesquely limited view of his duties, his complacent unconscious inadequacy, and his wrong priorities summarised by Elizabeth as 'his kind intention of christening, marrying, and burying his parishioners whenever it were required' (*PP*, 13). Henry Crawford in *Mansfield Park* is a more serious and revealing commentator who, feeling that the preaching of impressive and affecting sermons is the whole duty of an incumbent, and toying with the idea of what sort of a preacher he would himself make, points the reader towards the real duties of the real parish priest. By the light of Henry Crawford, we realise the duties Edmund Bertram undertakes in being ordained, and never judge him to be irresponsible or self-interested, even though he never proclaims his seriousness, still less a vocation. Sir Thomas Bertram, his father, is the only one who puts forward the duties of a parish priest, in terms so generalised (and thus very characteristic of their age, for which they had a weight they have since lost) that the modern reader may undervalue them:

'a parish has wants and claims which can be known only by a clergyman constantly resident, and which no proxy can be capable of satisfying to the same extent. Edmund might, in common phrase, do the duty of Thornton, that is, he might read prayers and preach, without giving up Mansfield Park; he might ride over, every Sunday, to a house nominally inhabited, and go through divine service; he might be clergyman of Thornton Lacy every seventh day, for three or four hours, if that would content him. But it will not. He knows that human nature needs more lessons than a weekly sermon can convey, and that if he does not live among his parishioners and prove himself by constant attention their well-wisher and friend, he does very little either for their good or his own'.

(*MP*, 25)

Clearly both Henry Crawford and Sir Thomas are in some way representative of their age. It is not easy to make generalisations about the late eighteenth-century clergyman, since there was comparatively little pressure exerted by the church itself, or by public opinion, to make the individual perform his office in a particular way—indeed very little to compel him to perform it at all. The most eccentric of eighteenth-century novelists, Laurence Sterne, was rector of Coxwold, in Yorkshire; and Patrick Brontë, father of the novelists and incumbent of the Yorkshire village of Haworth, began as a Methodist. If he wished, a rector could hire a curate and pay him a pittance to do his duty for him, and live elsewhere himself on the rest of what the living brought in. He could be a pluralist, and hold several livings at once, doing the duty of only one of them. Financially also there is a great deal of difference between clerics, and while the comfortably-off rector was more or less the equal of the landed gentry, some were crippled by a poverty as bad as any of their parishioners'. In 1811 there were nearly four thousand livings which brought in less than £150 a year, which, even with the different value of money then, is not adequate for a man with a family, living up to the standard a clergyman was expected to keep. With such incomes, pluralism was often a necessity.

The 'living'—the parish and the income that went with it—is not in the possession of the church, as it generally is now, by whom the rector is appointed, nor is it open to the congregation, as in Scotland, to bestow upon the man they choose. It is the possession usually of a landowner, or nobleman, to be bestowed by him upon the person of his choice. The value of these livings had risen generally (despite the grinding poverty which still obtained in some areas) and thus it came to seem both convenient and natural for the Church to become the profession, and the local living the property, of one of the sons of the man in whose gift it lay. The living is regarded as a practical asset, and a realisable one, as is proved in *Sense and Sensibility* by the surprise it causes Mr John Dashwood when Colonel Brandon offers one to the totally unconnected and unrelated Edward Ferrars:

> 'Really!—Well, this is very astonishing!—no relationship!—no connection between them!—and now that livings fetch such a price!—what was the value of this?'
> 'About two hundred a year.'
> 'Very well—and for the next presentation of that value— supposing the late incumbent to have been old and sickly, and likely to vacate it soon—he might have got, I dare say, fourteen hundred pounds.'

Colonel Brandon's living, while it enables Edward Ferrars to live independently of his tyrannous mother, is not considered, by the outspoken and practical Mrs Jennings, enough to live on when his wife can bring him no money of her own. 'Then they will have a child every year! And Lord help 'em! how poor they will be' (*SS*, 37) is a blunt but convincing estimate, when it is plain that Edward will be dragged down by an ignorant and vulgar wife, quite as much as by a small income.

Though the Church, like all other professions, can be bought and sold, and though such a system can be, and was, abused, by the man with no desire for holy living but only for what Gibbon called 'the fat slumbers of the Church', yet as Trevelyan points out, 'the religious needs of the village were served by a gentleman of education and refinement, though perhaps of no great zeal',[1] and the family group of the community's ruling house was kept together, and apathy may well be better than schism. Even pluralism may prove a good thing when one man had charge of two neighbouring parishes, neither of which could support a clergyman and the inevitable large family of the times. Jane

---

[1] *Illustrated English Social History* III, Chapter 2.

The rectory at Bingham's Molcombe, Dorset.

Austen silently presents the advantages, and her word must be weighed against the facts of historians and against the recollections and recreations of later writers. George Eliot, looking back almost to this age, draws the embittering lot of the poor parson in 'The Sad Fortunes of Amos Barton', the first of her *Scenes of Clerical Life*, while Thackeray's *Vanity Fair* recounts with comic gusto the hatreds in the Crawley family between the miserly and cunning Sir Pitt and his coarse, stupid, rector brother, Bute.

Clergymen are not so much separated from other men in other professions as they have been in both former and later periods of history. They cannot be identified, for one thing, by any difference in costume. Henry Tilney at Bath is only discovered to be one by Allen's enquiries; while Mary Crawford, hating the office yet in love with Edmund, writing to Fanny to tell her how good an impression Edmund has made on her fashionable friends in London, ends her letter: 'Luckily there is no distinction of dress now-a-days to tell tales, — but — but — but' (*MP*, 43). There is no restriction either on social behaviour, such as grew up with the evangelical movement and the Victorian period. Henry Tilney and Edmund Bertram both dance, for instance, Edmund plays cards for money, and the only one who sees any objection to doing so is the silly Mr Collins:

> 'I am by no means of opinion, I assure you,' said he, 'that a ball of this kind, given by a young man of character, can have any evil tendency; and I am so far from objecting to dancing myself that I shall hope to be honoured with the hands of all my fair cousins in the course of the evening.' (*PP*, 17)

Nearly all Jane Austen's men are 'gentlemen', and her novels occasionally suggest one of the obligations demanded of a gentleman in an age before Jane Austen's own; that of personally defending his honour against insult. Duelling had always been an aristocratic habit, even in its hey-day in the seventeenth and early eighteenth centuries. It is of course, illegal, and punishable, but it still occurs. By the time Jane Austen writes, duels are rare. There has been a great change of feeling since Sheridan, who, in *The Rivals*, can construct his last act upon a whole collection of affairs of honour between gentlemen. But still when honour is in question the duel is the obvious retaliation. Colonel Brandon, discovering that his ward has been seduced and deserted, sees no choice but to challenge Willoughby:

> 'When he returned to town, which was within a fortnight after myself, we met by appointment, he to defend, I to punish his conduct. We returned unwounded, and the meeting, therefore, never got abroad.'

Elinor sighed over the fancied necessity of this; but to a man and a soldier, she presumed not to censure it.

(*SS*, 30)

The suggestion here is that the men were going through the motions, rather than trying to kill; it is not likely that both of them would miss by accident. The other duel suggested in the novels is a comic thought, and may suggest that times are changing. In *Pride and Prejudice*, when Wickham has run off with Lydia, the only person who thinks that Mr Bennet's remedy is a duel is Mrs Bennet: 'I know he will fight Wickham, whenever he meets him, and then he will be killed, and what is to become of us all?' (*PP*, 47). Her lament changes when she thinks he is coming home:

'What, is he coming home, and without poor Lydia!' she cried. 'Sure, he will not leave London before he has found them. Who is to fight Wickham, and make him marry her, if he comes away?'

(*PP*, 48)

When Henry Crawford elopes with Maria Bertram (now Mrs Rushworth) in *Mansfield Park*, there is no suggestion that a duel would be in order, whether fought by injured husband or injured father.

CHAPTER FIVE

God and Mammon

THE English eighteenth century is often thought both material-
istic and irreligious. So is Jane Austen; and for many of the
same reasons, because she is practical about religion and money,
and does not theorise about either. Ethical principles accepted,
and codes of behaviour practised, or at least acknowledged, by a
larger part of the whole nation than ever before, make less stir
than those of an age of controversy. The seventeenth-century
philosopher Locke's arguments in favour of religious toleration
became accepted as the century went on, and Jane Austen, in her
letters, can express herself cautiously in favour of Evangelicalism:

> I am by no means convinced that we ought not all to be evan-
> gelicals, and am at least persuaded that they who are so from
> reason and feeling must be happiest and safest.
> (Letter to her niece Fanny Knight, 18 November 1814)

But Jane Austen thinks and works within the Church of England.
She never mentions Wesley or Methodism, even though to do so
would not have been inappropriate; any of her town communities
—say Meryton in *Pride and Prejudice* or *Emma's* Highbury—might
have had a Methodist chapel, or her secondary characters, like
Nurse Rooke in *Persuasion*, might have attended one. However,
'enthusiasm' of the sort experienced by Wesley's adherents is a
mainly lower-class, and industrial working-class, phenomenon,
mistrusted by the members of the professions and the gentry. A
later novelist who depicts the fervour of the time and its milieu is
Charlotte Brontë, writing in *Shirley* of the effect of the contemporary
economic upheavals upon the West Riding clothing districts of
Yorkshire, where Methodist fervour is attended with an
enthusiasm for machine-breaking.

Jane Austen, herself reticent, finds flippancy on religious
matters intolerable: she clearly judges her creation Mary

The domestic chapel at Ham House, Petersham.

Crawford, in *Mansfield Park*, very severely, and expects her readers so to judge her, when she makes cheap jokes in the private chapel at Sotherton, about family prayers:

> 'the young Mrs Eleanors and Mrs Bridgets—starched up into seeming piety, but with heads full of something very different— especially if the poor chaplain were not worth looking at—and, in those days, I fancy parsons were very inferior even to what they are now.'
>
> (*MP*, 9)

As the episode shows, Jane Austen is living at the beginning of an age of transition in morals and religion. Stable and moderate though she seems, there are signs of the change here, for the chapel is of another and earlier age, when the master met his whole household for morning and evening prayers. Mary is the modern voice when she says, 'every body likes to go their own way—to choose their own time and manner of devotion' (*ibid.*) and although Edmund disagrees with her—'Do you think the minds which are suffered, which are indulged in wanderings in a chapel, would be more collected in a closet?' (*ibid.*)—his is the lone voice, while hers assumes general agreement.

Jane Austen, like the century, grows more serious with age. In *Persuasion*, her last novel, Mr Elliot is suspect of 'Sunday travelling'. No such grounds of disapproval occur in the earlier novels, although it would be difficult to prove that Jane Austen ever condones it, by allowing a character to travel on the Sabbath. Her clergymen grow more scrupulous and strict. She never excuses an irreligious or irresponsible one—she never excuses anyone irreligious or irresponsible—but her earliest cleric, Henry Tilney, holidaying at Bath and living half his time away from his parish, behaves in a way impossible to her later one, Edmund Bertram, who is, like him, the son of a wealthy country land-owner. One must remember of course that the main purpose of *Northanger Abbey* is literary burlesque of novels of gothic horror and excessive sentiment, and that Henry Tilney is made a clergyman partly because it is an unromantic, and un-novel-like profession for a hero, so as to expose the improbabilities of the novels Jane Austen is ridiculing; whereas *Mansfield Park*, she said once, is about 'ordination'.[1] Edward Ferrars in *Sense and Sensibility*, though no part of a burlesque like Henry Tilney, is still closer to him than to Edmund. The novel's avowed purpose is to expound principles of conduct and a proper combination of good sense and right feeling. Edward Ferrars has both, as well as a strong sense of honour, which chains him to his engagement to a worthless girl, even when his mother disinherits and disowns him. Yet he accepts Colonel Brandon's gift of a living with no sign that he thinks of the Church as anything more than an appropriate occupation for a quiet, reserved, and intelligent young man.

With secondary characters the change may be even more accurately charted. Mr Collins is the first. He is obviously ill-qualified for the Church by being ill-qualified to be a rational man; he is, as Elizabeth says, pompous, narrow-minded, and silly. Though Jane Austen is decisive about his fallings-off, he is

---

[1] Letter to Cassandra Austen, Friday 29 January 1813.

too comic and too grotesque to carry great weight. His first letter to Mr Bennet exposes his farcically wrong priorities, putting his duty to his patron, Lady Catherine, before even *his* very limited notion of his duties to his parish:

> 'it shall be my earnest endeavour to demean myself with grateful respect towards her ladyship, and be ever ready to perform those rites and ceremonies which are instituted by the Church of England.'
>
> *(PP*, 13)

Equally satirically self-exposing is his comment on the rumour that Elizabeth and Darcy are engaged: he warns Mr Bennet that Lady Catherine disapproves, and that Elizabeth 'should not run hastily into a marriage that has not been properly sanctioned' *(PP*, 57)—not by the Church, but by Lady Catherine. By the time she writes *Mansfield Park*, Jane Austen has changed. Dr Grant, rector of Mansfield, no fool like Mr Collins, little seen in the action, is yet a more serious and revealing type of cleric. He performs his duties adequately and without parade, but is far more harshly judged, out of the mouth of Mary Crawford, who is so often the voice of worldly standards:

> 'Though Dr Grant is most kind and obliging to me, and though he is really a gentleman, and I dare say a good scholar and clever, and often preaches good sermons, and is very respectable, *I* see him to be an indolent selfish bon vivant, who must have his palate consulted in everything, who will not stir a finger for the convenience of anyone, and who, moreover, if the cook makes a blunder, is out of humour with his excellent wife.'
>
> *(MP*, 11)

It is conversely the right-thinking Fanny who comes to his defence, in defending his office.

Jane Austen's allusion to evangelicalism has already been mentioned. There are two other small, but significant, signs of the times. One is Mary Crawford's frivolous guess that Edmund stays at his parish because there may be 'some old woman at Thorntom Lacey to be converted' *(MP*, 40), for 'conversion' in this sense is a tenet of methodism and nonconformity; the other is the remark by Mrs Elton in *Emma*, who, when Jane Fairfax alludes to employment agencies as 'offices for the sale—not quite of human flesh—

but of human intellect', ridiculously midunderstands and replies,

> 'Oh, my dear, human flesh! You quite shock me; if you mean a
> fling at the slave trade, I assure you Mr Suckling was always rather
> a friend to the abolition.'

(E, 35)

Anti-slavery was a cause which brought together all low church-
men—evangelicals, non-conformists, free-thinkers and Unitarians
alike. The Slave Trade was abolished in 1807, and the campaign
to free all slaves in the British Empire went on vigorously thereafter, even though it was unsuccessful until 1833.

While Jane Austen feels she can take for granted the eternal
verities, she knows that where money is concerned it is her business
as a social novelist to be precise and to make discriminations. She
is unusually explicit, for a novelist, about money matters—though
only within her own precisely chosen range. Her concern with
money is solely as one of the many matters which determine how
life shall be lived, so she generally refers to the personal income
accruing from land, from livings, or from other professions,

Coins of the reign of George III (actual size). (1) A Bank of England
'dollar': (2) a quarter sovereign: (3) a crown: (4) a half sovereign.

considered as a means of providing for a home and family. Even within her middle-class range she errs rather on the side of caution, when one recollects that clergymen contrived, though with great difficulty, to live on incomes of £100 a year. Isabella Thorpe in *Northanger Abbey* can condemn £400 a year as 'an income hardly enough to find one in the common necessaries of life' (*NA*, 17). She is exaggerating because she has been disappointed, expecting that her betrothed would prove to be worth much more. Yet the sensible Elinor Dashwood in *Sense and Sensibility*, at last engaged to Edward Ferrars, is not 'quite enough in love to think that three hundred and fifty pounds a year would supply them with the comforts of life' (*SS*, 48). The important word here is 'comforts'. People could, and did, live on very much less—in the country, farming land either freehold or rented, it was still possible to be so nearly self-supporting as to require money hardly at all. The novelist Peacock, in *Melincourt* (1817), routs an exponent of the doctrines of Malthus (on the dangers of over-population) with a richly comic rustic couple who are prepared to marry on fourteen shillings a week:

> 'And Zukey here ha' laid up a mint o' money: she wur dairy-maid at Varmer Cheescurd's, and ha' gotten vour pounds zeventeen shill'n's and ninepence in t'old chest wi' three vlat locks and a padlock.'
>
> (*Melincourt*, 34)

This marriage is plainly a risky business, but not at all an improbable one. Jane Austen errs on the side of prudence and comfort perhaps, but figures given with such confidence and accuracy as hers, and never questioned by her contemporary readers, are obviously accurate, and meant to be attended to. One of the most important conversations about money is between Elinor and Marianne Dashwood, the representatives respectively of good sense and ill-judging enthusiasm; Marianne exclaims,

> 'What have wealth or grandeur to do with happiness?'
>
> 'Grandeur has but little,' said Elinor, 'but wealth has much to do with it.'
>
> 'Elinor, for shame!' said Marianne; 'money can only give happiness where there is nothing else to give it. Beyond a competence, it can afford no real satisfaction, as far as mere self is concerned.'

'Perhaps,' said Elinor, smiling, 'we may come to the same point. *Your* competence and *my* wealth are very much alike, I dare say; and without them, as the world goes now, we shall both agree that every kind of external comfort must be wanting. Your ideas are only more noble than mine. Come, what is your competence?'

'About eighteen hundred or two thousand a year; not more than *that.*'

Elinor laughed. '*Two* thousand a year! *One* is my wealth! I guessed how it would end.'

'And yet two thousand a year is a very moderate income,' said Marianne. 'A family cannot well be maintained on a smaller. I am sure I am not extravagant in my demands. A proper establishment of servants, a carriage, perhaps two, and hunters, cannot be supported on less.'

(*SS*, 17)

In *Mansfield Park*, Jane Austen has moved financially upwards: Henry Crawford estimates Edmund Bertram's assets, evidently justly:

'He will have a very pretty income to play ducks and drakes with, and earned without much trouble. I apprehend he will not have less than seven hundred a year. Seven hundred a year is a fine thing for a younger brother; and as of course he will live at home, it will be all for his *menus plaisirs.*'

while his sister's reply throws light on his own:

'You would look rather blank, Henry, if your *menus plaisirs* were to be limited to seven hundred a year.'

(*MP*, 37)

The only really fantastic figure Jane Austen offers is for the novels' most conventionally romantic character, Mr Darcy, who has ten thousand a year.

'It is a truth universally acknowledged,' says the famous opening sentence of *Pride and Prejudice*, 'that a single man in possession of a good fortune, must be in want of a wife.' Marriage, in Jane Austen, is closely bound up with money. It could not mean, to a reader in Jane Austen's own time, what it means to a reader today. Jane Austen's own attitude to money and marriage should be clear to any intelligent reader, being voiced through her heroines, particularly Elinor Dashwood. The attitudes of her other characters vary, and reflect, not their author, but types of human nature and aspects of their age. Marriage is a social contract, and so entails social obligations. In an age where there are no social services, no insurance schemes, no national medical care, no pensions schemes for sickness or old age; where large families are the norm, and where divorce is virtually out of the question, a man who marries commits himself to heavy responsibilities, and the woman who marries stakes the rest of her life on his performance of them. An adequate income is not merely desirable, it is vital. Hence a very reasonable concern on everyone's part with the assets of a possible suitor, and the fortune of a possible wife. The topic is so important that it constantly recurs, to the distaste of those who do not realise how central it must be to novels which frame their deep moral concerns on the events leading to a young woman's marriage. The most explicit discussions of money in matrimony are those in *Pride and Prejudice* and *Persuasion*, both of which depend upon how the characters weigh the rival claims of prudence and feeling. In *Pride and Prejudice*, Elizabeth's friend Charlotte Lucas, as already mentioned, is the voice of cold prudence:

> Without thinking highly either of men or of matrimony, marriage had always been her object; it was the only honourable provision for well-educated young women of small fortune, and however uncertain of giving happiness, must be their pleasantest preservative from want.
>
> (PP, 22)

A more powerful, because more detached and impartial, voice of reason is Elizabeth's aunt Mrs Gardiner, who warns her against falling in love with Wickham, because he has no apparent means:

> 'Do not involve yourself, or endeavour to involve him, in an affection which the want of fortune would make so very imprudent. I have nothing to say against *him*; he is a most interesting young man; and if he had the fortune he ought to have, I think you could not do better. But as it is—you must not let your fancy run away with you. You have sense, and we all expect you to use it.'
>
> (PP, 26)

Elizabeth does. She eschews Wickham; but on the other hand she is not for a moment tempted to accept Darcy when he first proposes, for the sake of his ten thousand a year. The dilemma in *Persuasion* is almost the reverse. Anne is wrongly persuaded to break off her engagement to Frederick Wentworth because the young sailor has only the prospect, possibly distant, of an income before him. Eight years later,

> she felt that were any young person, in similar circumstances, to apply to her for counsel, they would never receive any of such certain immediate wretchedness, such uncertain future good.
>
> (*P*, 4)

That money is taken seriously by persons whose sense Jane Austen has taught us to respect appears in a casual remark made by the sensible Mrs Weston (Emma's former governess, and Frank's stepmother) of Frank Churchill's engagement to Jane Fairfax: 'It is not a connexion to gratify' (*E*, 46) she remarks, even though the penniless Jane has proved herself far more estimable than her irresponsible fiancé. Similarly Mr Knightley takes a very practical view of Harriet Smith's matrimonial chances:

> 'What are Harriet Smith's claims, either of birth, nature, or education, to any connection higher than Robert Martin [a young farmer]? . . . I felt, that as to fortune, in all probability he might do much better; and that as to a rational companion or useful helpmate, he could not do worse.'

Blunter, less subtle utterances of the popular view abound, such as the caustic opening of *Mansfield Park*:

> About thirty years ago, Miss Maria Ward of Huntingdon, with only seven thousand pounds, had the good luck to captivate Sir Thomas Bertram. . . . All Huntingdon exclaimed on the greatness of the match, and her uncle, the lawyer, himself, allowed her to be at least three thousand pounds short of any equitable claim to it.

But it is always clear from her tone that the author, like Catherine Morland, hates 'the idea of one great fortune looking out for another' (*NA*, 15).

Settlements are often mentioned in connection with weddings. They are made by the father upon the daughter, as Mr Bennet has to commit himself to settling £1,000 on Lydia, to induce Wickham to marry her. The settlement is of course the legal handing over of the dowry, but may also be the means by which the wife is enabled to have some money of her own. This is plainly the meaning in Sheridan's *School for Scandal*, when Sir Peter Teazle, momentarily in a good humour with his wife, promises, 'You shall no longer reproach me with not giving you an independent settlement' (Act III, scene 1). If no settlement is made, all her monies become legally her husband's. Until the Married Women's Property Act of 1882, a wife had no legal financial rights of her own, and no way of preventing her husband from using or losing their money in any way he chose; hence Darcy's horror (apart from natural affection) when Wickham almost manages to elope with his young sister Georgiana: 'Mr Wickham's object was unquestionably my sister's fortune, which is thirty thousand pounds' (*PP*, 12).

Parents' permission is considered necessary to a marriage, but, provided the young people are of age, is a formality rather than a requisite. Elizabeth, hearing that her father has received a letter, wonders whether Mr Darcy has made a formal offer for her, and 'was undetermined whether to be pleased that he has explained himself at all, or offended that the letter was not addressed to herself' (*PP*, 57). Generally the lady is asked first, and the parents only when the matter is settled. Arranged marriages are things of the past, the only one mentioned in the novels being the disastrous one in *Sense and Sensibility* which forces Colonel Brandon's childhood sweetheart to marry his brother: not only is the marriage a generation back, but Jane Austen may well be drawing upon literature rather than from life when she invents it.

Though the preliminaries to marriage are more elaborate than now, weddings are less so. They are not great celebrations, either for the pair or for their friends and neighbours. Charlotte Lucas and Mr Collins are quite representative in leaving Longbourn, for their home at Hunsford, literally from the church door. What few celebrations are mentioned impinge on the character who is the most distressed—Mr Woodhouse in *Emma* for instance, when Miss Taylor marries Mr Weston:

What was unwholesome to him, he regarded as unfit for anybody; and he had, therefore, earnestly tried to dissuade them from having any wedding-cake at all.

(*E*, 2)

Less celebration means less preparation. All that are mentioned are clothes and carriages, and even these generally reveal trivial-minded people. Mrs Bennet 'was more alive to the disgrace, which the want of new clothes must reflect on her daughter's nuptials, than to any sense of shame at her eloping and living with Wickham, a fortnight before they took place' (*PP*, 50). In *Mansfield Park* the neighbourhood is alive to the disgrace of Mr Rushworth's using 'the same chaise which [he] had used a twelve-month before' (*MP*, 21). Even the wealthy Mr Rushworth and his bride go straight to Mr Rushworth's home at Sotherton, with no suggestion of a honeymoon or bridal tour. They exemplify also another changed custom: Maria takes her sister Julia with her. One could suppose that this is a peculiar case (since the wife might well welcome a relief from her stupid husband) except that Mrs Jennings, in *Sense and Sensibility*, blames Lucy Steele for being so unkind as to leave her sister behind, when she marries Robert Ferrars and drives off to Dawlish; this too is more a flight from the wrath of Mrs Ferrars, than a honeymoon. The only character who seems to have one is Emma, who makes her first visit to the sea.

Marriages, as now, were by banns, or by licence from the bishop. The licence costs more and has a *cachet* proved by Mrs Bennet: 'A special licence. You must and shall be married by a special licence' (*PP*, 59), is part of her delight that Elizabeth is to marry Darcy.

Divorce is a near-impossibility. Only the husband can obtain one, and then only by Act of Parliament, and only if he is wealthy: like Mr Rushworth in *Mansfield Park* who, when his wife Maria has gone off with Henry Crawford

> was released from the engagement to be mortified and unhappy, till some other pretty girl could attract him to matrimony again, and he might set forward on a second, and it is to be hoped, more prosperous trial of the state.
>
> (*MP*, 48)

Legal separations are also possible for both men and women, and easier, available on various grounds, including physical violence. But they do not permit remarriage, nor concern Jane Austen.

Death, that other great terminus of human affairs, plays but a small part in Jane Austen's novels. One of the very few people to die in the course of the actions is Mrs Churchill in *Emma*, who is known to the reader only by the report of other characters. Illnesses, of various sorts, are another, and not uncommon, matter.

Three things make the importance of such illnesses difficult to assess: one is the general truth that any sort of ill-health was more uncomfortable, and more dangerous, in an age when medicine was still partly guesswork, tradition, and superstition; when the nature of most infections was unknown and hygiene rudimentary; when asepsis was unheard-of and surgery of any sort more often fatal than not; and when medical care was that of the local apothecary, whose profession was considered not much above a trade. Another difficulty is that illnesses were confused and known by quite different names, so that Jane Austen's terminology is not always clear. A third is that many of the illnesses which Jane Austen's contemporaries feared, and of which they died, are now either almost non-existent or are easily controlled by vaccination, immunisation, or drugs. Jane Austen is sparing in her allusions to illness and disease, although, as a clergyman's daughter brought by her position into daily contact with those around her, she must have known of all the hazards to life and health. Although she wisely does not offer any sensational or unusual diseases or disasters, such as would be out of place in these least sensational of novels, it is easy for the modern reader to underestimate even the few dangers which do beset her characters. In general Jane Austen merely defines the symptoms, where the modern novelist would identify the disease; hence the impression that nearly all those who fall ill—Marianne Dashwood, Jane Bennet, Harriet Smith—have nothing worse than a cold. Many menaces lie behind so simple a symptom as a sore throat—two of the commonest being influenza and diphtheria, both of them quite often fatal. It is plain that Marianne Dashwood at Cleveland, who has neglected herself for weeks before catching a chill, 'heavy and feverish, with a pain in her limbs, a cough and a sore throat' (*SS*, 41) would be seriously ill even today, and is very seriously ill indeed in an age with no antibiotics. There is nothing alarmist or foolish in Mrs Palmer's leaving home to avoid, for herself and her new baby, a quite possibly fatal infection. Other illnesses mentioned are scarlet fever and measles (both dangerous), and that ailment characteristic of an age of heavy drinkers, gout; the last has one of the pleasantest remedies offered for it—Constantia wine (*SS*, 29).

One illness that was on the way to disappearing was smallpox. At the beginning of the eighteenth century it was prevalent, frequently mortal, and almost always disfiguring. Inoculation, introduced from Turkey, by, amongst others, the well-known *bel esprit* Lady Mary Wortley Montague, had made some headway; and vaccination, discovered at the end of the century by Jenner, arrested finally a disease that had hitherto carried off a thirteenth of each generation.

The amount of concern for the health of women at childbirth, and for babies and small children, is surprisingly little when one considers that most parents could expect to lose one child at least in a lifetime, and that two of Jane Austen's brothers lost their wives, one of them after the birth of her twelfth child. In the novels, though Mr Woodhouse undoubtedly may worry too much about the health of all his acquaintance, he undoubtedly has great cause for worry; while Mrs Palmer, when her baby 'cried and fretted, and was all over pimples' (*SS*, 36), may well have mistrusted her robust mother's diagnosis of teething rash—or, as she expresses it, 'nothing in the world but the red-gum' (*ibid*.).

Jane Austen's own views on health and medicine, one gathers from the letters, are very much those of most unscientific people of her time, robust and practical, and based on common sense and observation, on avoiding medical interference where possible, and trusting to familiar remedies which, if little use, are equally no harm. She is neither superstitious nor sentimental, and her good sense comes out in her sensible characters: when Jane Fairfax comes back, obviously out of health, to Highbury in winter instead of going with her friends to Ireland, Emma is very right in thinking that health is not the reason (though of course she turns out to be grotesquely wrong about the real reason):

'As to the pretence of trying her native air, I look upon that as a mere excuse.—In the summer it might have passed; but what can any body's native air do for them in the months of January, February, and March? Good fires and carriages would be much more to the purpose in most cases of delicate health, and I dare say in her's.' (*E*, 26)

'The Consultation, or Last Hope', by Thomas Rowlandson.

In medicine as in other matters, Jane Austen's is an age of change. There had been considerable advances in medicine in the later part of the eighteenth century, and consequently a lowered death-rate and a growing population. The great centres for surgery and medicine are London and Edinburgh, whence new methods spread by degrees to other towns and country districts, and to the poor, as the men trained at the medical schools went out into practice, and ousted gradually old remedies based on superstitions and folklore. Health was the care of the surgeon, the physician, the apothecary, and the unlicensed practitioner. Hartfield in *Emma*, almost a small town, is quite representative in having only the apothecary Mr Perry, who is its only representative of medical science. His profession is not highly thought of, and it is his personal qualities that make him the trusted adviser and friend of the leading gentleman Mr Woodhouse, who, however, significantly calls him simply 'Perry', without any 'mister'. His advice is all sound sense—as was probably that of many of his kind—and was thus at any rate as near to science as to superstition. The apothecary ranks lower than the physician, who also is represented in *Emma*, by Mr Wingfield, the favourite of Mr Woodhouse's London-dwelling daughter Isabella. Neither avocation ranked high among professions, for which the training was by apprenticeship, as to a trade, as is also surgery, which is one that in 1810–14, when Jane Austen was bringing out her first three novels, was proving uncongenial to John Keats.

Medical men are never called doctors by Jane Austen— although the meaning does occur in Johnson's Dictionary (1755). She uses the term only for clergymen, a usage that remains well into the nineteenth century. The 'Doctor' in *Sense and Sensibility*, about whom Anne Steele so much relishes being teased, is clerical, not medical.

CHAPTER SIX

The Squire and His Relations

JANE Austen's England is England in its last years as a land
founded upon farming, the village community, and the small
town. Although an industrial society was rapidly growing up in
the North Midlands and the North, the South, of which she writes,
and in which lived the greater part of the population, is still
agricultural. Jane Austen therefore does not distort the contemporary scene when she omits such new and exciting happenings as
form the substance of Charlotte Brontë's *Shirley*. What can be seen
in retrospect is not what is seen by the contemporary. Likewise the
order and tradition of village life are taken for granted by Jane
Austen and her contemporaries: it is only the nostalgia of the
backward look, when things are vanished or vanishing, that
emphasises them, as Hardy does, who in *The Trumpet Major* looks
back to Jane Austen's own time and writes of what is close to Jane
Austen's own country. For Jane Austen herself, social order is
natural, and requires no explanation.

The country, if one includes in this all except the largest cities, is
still the home of four-fifths of the population, that is, about
7,200,000 people. The life Jane Austen writes of is therefore not so
much that of a minority as it sometimes seems to be to the modern
reader. This is also the age of a fast-enlarging middle class, many
of whom, while spending some of their time in the city, had their
homes outside it. There were many who, like Mr Bingley, rented a
house and some land which they did not wish or could not afford
to buy; or who, like the Crawfords or Jane Austen herself, were
free to spend long periods in visits to relations who lived in the
country, whether as clergy like the Crawfords' sister and brother-
in-law, the Grants, or as landowners like Jane Austen's own brother
Edward. Such people are in the happy state of being thoroughly at
home, but being detached enough to be conscious of the excellence
and beauty of their surroundings. This is the age not only of the

The greenhouses of a 'forcing garden' in winter.

cult of the picturesque (which is rather different, and will be dealt with later), but of the passion for general improvement in farming and gardening, and of a delight in familiar landscape in art; it is the age of the great English water-colourists—Girtin, Wilson, Cotman, and Turner—and of their thousands of followers and pupils, both professional and amateur.

The English landscape at the opening of the nineteenth century was not unlike what it still is today, where urban spread and housing schemes have not obscured it. Most villages have their church and manor house, which in turn has its park, laid out according to the rules, if not actually with the assistance, of the great landscape gardeners of the late eighteenth century; such parks were in their prime, with their trees and shrubs carefully trimmed and planted and at their best. Surrounding lands were also shaped by man's purposes, well populated but not at all crowded. The enclosures of the large open fields of earlier ages meant that land was now thoroughly and efficiently cultivated, with a beauty that comes from order and fitness, such as Edward Ferrars finds to approve when he visits Devon, and so disappoints

Marianne Dashwood with his very just, though unimpassioned, praise:

> 'I call it a very fine country—the hills are steep, the woods seem full of fine timber, and the valley looks comfortable and snug— with rich meadows and several neat farm houses scattered here and there. It exactly answers my idea of a fine country, because it unites beauty with utility—and I dare say it is a picturesque one, because you admire it.'
>
> (*SS*, 18)

Edward Ferrars has plainly much in common with William Cobbett, who, most practical of men, yet praises Hertfordshire in these terms:

> you go on from field to field, the sort of corn, the sort of undergrowth and timber, the shape and size of the fields, the height of the hedge- rows, the height of the trees, all continually varying. Talk of pleasure-grounds, indeed! What that man ever invented under the name of pleasure-grounds can equal these fields of Hertfordshire?

The nature of the landscape is determined by the uses to which it is put, for in the greater part of southern and midland England it is by now all under use, and generally for mixed farming. The richest lands are used either for corn-growing, whose stubble is then used to feed pigs, or for rich pasture for cows; the sparser downlands support sheep. The whole has the sense of discipline and order that, even fifty years before, seems so surprisingly lacking when one reads *Tom Jones*, where journeys through the west and south of England cover extensive tracts which are both wild and dangerous.

This is the age of the Agricultural Revolution, with the great enclosures of open fields—of which each individual had cultivated his own share—and of commons—on which commoners had grazed their own few sheep or cattle. With enclosure, farming became more scientific, and much more efficient. Jane Austen's own county, Hampshire, was one of the earliest to be enclosed and farmed, and so in her time suffered few changes. One of the few allusions to one of the most extensive changes of her time is a complaint in *Sense and Sensibility* from Mr John Dashwood of how 'the enclosure of Norland Common [in Sussex] now carrying on, is a most serious drain' (*SS*, 32) on his income. Generally speaking, the impression in the novels is of the country, and country life, as a settled, rather than a changing thing—an interesting instance of the difference between how an age may seem to a social historian and to one who lives in it. The good landlord is almost by definition also a farmer, and living within this revolution. Landlords could not resist enclosures, which were enforced by a succession of Acts of Parliament in the reign of George III between 1760 and 1820. The result was the increase in large estates, from which farms were leased to tenants, who in turn employed landless labourers (like the optimistic rustic couple, already mentioned, in Peacock's *Melincourt*). This is the way in which Mr Darcy's large estate at Pemberley would be conducted, and the way in which we have glimpses of Mr Knightley running Donwell.

New methods were being introduced into almost all branches of farming: draining land, drilling, sowing, manuring, breeding and feeding cattle, making roads and farm buildings, as well as into scientific methods of rotation of crops and pasture. The results are enormously increased yields, both of crops and of fat stock. Farmers therefore now produce more and more for sale at the local market-town, not merely for their own and their household's subsistence. The whole nation becomes healthier and better fed, not only because yields of corn are greater, but because, with the growing of root crops on which cattle could be fed all winter instead of slaughtered in the autumn, fresh meat becomes available all the year round.

The darker side of the picture is one Jane Austen does not concern herself with, even though it is one that affects the southern counties of England in particular. This is the rise in the number of farm labourers who, after enclosure, own no land of their own, but whose wages as the employees of others do not rise in proportion to the general prosperity; they inevitably either become paupers, or leave the country, in hopes of doing better in the towns, and begin the great nineteenth-century shift of population to the cities.

In her novels Jane Austen wisely draws on the lasting qualities of country life rather than its transient ones. Her novels, although accurate in their chronology within themselves, are not of particular years or periods. They contain no datable historical events. *Persuasion*, the only one in which the dates of events are given, concentrates most of all upon the recurring, and therefore timeless, aspects of the countryside. One of Jane Austen's few idyllic passages is that in which Anne Elliot enjoys an autumn walk :

> after another half-mile of gradual ascent through large enclosures,
> the ploughs at work, and the fresh-made path spoke the farmer,
> counteracting the sweets of poetical despondence, and meaning to
> have spring again.
>
> <div align="right">(<i>P</i>, 10)</div>

Neither here nor elsewhere does Jane Austen give a hint of what
must have been one of the pressing questions in the mind of any of
her farming gentlemen, the price of wheat. This rose from 43*s*. a
quarter in 1792, before the wars against Napoleon began, to 126*s*.
in 1812, when foreign corn had become scarce, and when
Napoleon advanced on Moscow. The poor suffered and farmers
prospered; but after the war, when prices slumped, many farmers
were ruined. Jane Austen, in a farming community, heard and
saw it all, as small remarks in the letters bear witness, and one may
detect her knowledge in the sad case of old John Abdy in *Emma*,
who, Miss Bates tells us,

> 'was clerk to my poor father twenty-seven years; and now, poor
> old man, he is bed-ridden, and very poorly with the rheumatic gout
> in his joints . . . And poor John's son came to talk to Mr Elton about
> relief from the parish : he is very well to do himself, being head man
> at the Crown, ostler, and every thing of that sort, but still he cannot
> keep his father without some help.'
>
> <div align="right">(<i>E</i>, 44)</div>

Even the passing of the Corn Laws in 1815, though it helped the
farmer by fixing the price of corn, did not help much. John Abdy
and his son reveal another and older problem, that created by not
raising wages in relation to the cost of living but supplementing
inadequate wages out of the parish rate. Jane Austen has her eyes
open to the hardships suffered outside what she chooses to make
her subject and presumes her reader has his open too. He cannot
learn from her about the Corn Laws or the system of parish relief,
but he may misread her if not aware of them.

On the whole, farmers at this period flourish and prosper,
whether tenant or yeoman, and could afford to educate their
families better—as Robert Martin's sister Elizabeth was educated
at the same school as Harriet Smith—to indulge in some of the
amusements of gentlemen, like hunting, and to fill their houses

with the appurtenances of genteel comfort, like upholstery on their chairs, carpets on their floors, and Wedgwood pottery instead of pewter.

Closely linked to farming is food. Better agriculture is followed by better nutrition, but, on the other hand, war puts up prices, and the ban on foreign corn makes the home product, if not scarce, expensive. The price of many things rose steadily. Sugar, for instance, rose from eightpence to one shilling and fourpence per loaf, and other supplies, though only indirectly affecting food, rose likewise: hay from two guineas a load to seven pounds, oats from ten shillings a quarter to two guineas. Most of the necessaries of life quadrupled in price in thirty years. As the price of bread increased, so did the fear of famine, and with both, in large towns and particularly London, went the threat of riots, a threat made the greater by there being as yet no police force. Resentment was directed especially against dealers suspected of making a profit out of the general want by forestalling the market: that is, buying up produce in order to resell immediately at a high price, or in order to hold it back until prices became even higher.

Generalisations about conditions are difficult, as they vary within quite short periods, according to prices, war and weather, and according to district. Southern and Eastern England, which Jane Austen knew best, suffered the least hardship, although other parts, notably the manufacturing districts of Lancashire and Yorkshire, fared badly. No-one in an area like Jane Austen's starved. But she is aware of the discomforts of a small income. Miss Bates's household, although far above that of the farm labourer, is yet dependent on Mr Knightley's generosity for apples to bake for old Mrs Bates, and on the Woodhouse's for probably a fair part of their fresh meat: Emma sends them a hind-quarter of a pig, which would go a long way, salted, for an old woman, a middle-aged one, a sickly young one, and their maid, who is the only one likely to have a hearty appetite. They depend on Emma again for the arrowroot for the invalid Jane, and it is a measure of Jane's bitterness towards Emma that she rejects the gift.

One of the most entertaining sources of evidence for late eighteenth-century eating habits is Parson Woodforde, exceptional though he plainly was in his passion for food. Though one may safely assume that many parsons, perhaps most, did not eat so well or so copiously, it is known that the English in general were reputed to eat well in his time, especially of meat. William Hazlitt the essayist, never a wealthy man, imagining a desirable supper after a day's walking, envisages 'eggs and a rasher, a rabbit smothered in onions, or a veal-cutlet'[1]; while the engraver Thomas Bewick, as a boy in Northumberland, had salmon at three halfpence a pound. Parson Woodforde himself records some memorable meals, such as, for seven visitors,

> some Skaite and Oyster Sauce, Knuckle of Veal and a Tongue, a fine Fore Quarter of Lamb and plumb Pudding. 2nd. Course, Asparagus, Lobster, Raspberry Tartlets, black Caps set into Custard etc. We had also Cucumbers and Radishes.

(*The Diary of a Country Parson*, 1758–1802, entry for 17 April 1787)

Visitors to the country, however, were not always pleased with the cookery. A German pastor Carl Moritz does not relish his mid-day meal of half-boiled or half-roasted meat, cabbage-leaves boiled in plain water, and a sauce made of flour and butter, the usual way of dressing vegetables. Underdone meat seems to be an English taste: Jane Austen mentions that 'the strength of our dinner was a boiled leg of mutton, underdone even for James [her brother]'[2] By contrast a labourer's diet was much sparser, consisting of bread, butter, cheese, pickled pork, and a little butcher's meat. Beer was expensive, and beginning to be replaced by sweetened tea. In cities, among the prosperous, this is an age both of heavy eating and drinking and of ostentatious extravagance. In London in 1827 cocks' combs were sold at 22s. a pound, of which a pound and a half were needed to make a dish.

It is remarkable to anyone who knows the age from other sources how little Jane Austen mentions drink and drunkenness in her works. The eighteenth century had been perhaps the heaviest drinking one in English history, and not only for the rich. The worst of the era of gin-drinking was over before she was born. An Act of 1751, taxing spirits and preventing their retail sale, had put a stop to the drinking of gin instead of beer by the poor which

---

[1] 'On Going a Journey', *Table Talk*.
[2] Letter to Cassandra Austen, Wednesday 7 January 1807.

had resulted, between 1740 and 1742, in the burials in London being twice as many as the baptisms. Even so, heavy drinking of wines was usual, and not at all disapproved by many. Dr Grant, rector of Mansfield, is a survivor of the old school who rejoices that 'Mr Crawford's being his guest was an excuse for drinking claret every day' (*MP*, 5); and *Northanger Abbey* also harks back to an earlier state of things, with John Thorpe bragging of how much was drunk at Oxford:

> 'it was reckoned a remarkable thing at the last party in my rooms, that upon average we cleared about five pints a head.'   (*NA*, 9)

and suggesting that Mr Allen 'drinks his bottle a-day' (*ibid.*). While such quantities seem formidable and undoubtedly could be (and were) dangerous in the long run, yet one should remember that wines then were not fortified with spirits as they are now, and would therefore not be so potent. Drink and disorder go together in literature just as in life. Although Jane Austen, unlike her eighteenth-century predecessors Fielding and Smollet and even Fanny Burney, avoids dealing with scenes of riotise, the effects of drink taken in the dining-room after dinner, which might well be detected by the ladies in the drawing-room dispensing tea and coffee, never are so detected in Jane Austen. The only character who is even suspected of having taken too much is Mr Elton, who having had 'too much of Mr Weston's good wine' proposes rashly and presumptuously to Emma, in the carriage taking them home from the Weston's Christmas Party.

Although tea and coffee are supplanting ale, beer, wines and spirits as family drinks, they have by no means taken over entirely. Fanny Price is given wine and water for her headache at supper-time, and Elinor drinks the old Constantia wine offered to Marianne as comfort for a broken heart.

If people's wages and food vary, so do the places in which they live. The rural scene of the time contains several quite clearly distinguishable sorts of dwelling. At the bottom of the scale comes the cottage, the dwelling of all those below the ranks which keep servants, and of the lowest sort of those who do. These ranks, although those which Jane Austen of choice excludes from her novels, were the greater number of rural householders.

'Old Cottage,' by John Crome.

The cottage comprises, at bottom, the bare essentials for living: a living-room (in many districts called, simply, the 'house'), a fire with some means of cooking, a place for preparing food, places for storing it and for washing, and a sleeping area. Such cottages are often old, dating from a hundred years back and more, since a cottage, once built, is kept in the family (if freehold) or passed on from tenant to tenant (often also of the same family) if owned by a landlord. The nineteenth-century labourer might often live in a Queen Anne, or even a Jacobean, cottage, just as the modern one often lives in a Victorian house. Cottages are generally small, mainly so as to be easier to keep heated, and made of local materials which vary in different parts of the country. In Jane Austen's Hampshire they are generally brick. By the nineteenth century the downstairs floor is properly surfaced, with bricks or flags at worst, and wood at best. The upstairs room, or rooms, is wood, of course, and reached either by a narrow stairway from the downstairs room, or by a ladder.

Furniture is at a minimum. This is before the days of the mass-produced article, and things are locally made, to local patterns. Downstairs furnishings are a table and plain chairs and stools of wood, with a dresser or wall-cupboard; upstairs, a curtained bed and a linen chest. Furniture also lasted often more than a lifetime and was handed down, particularly such more treasured items as the linen-chest—into which category may come Sukey's old chest already mentioned, 'wi' three vlat locks and a padlock', containing four pounds seventeen shillings and ninepence.

Increasing prosperity among the merchant classes, and the growing taste for the picturesque, lead to a fashionable taste for the cottage and what can be done with it. Towns are small enough for men of business to live on their outskirts, while big enough to make them wish not to live in the centre. So develops the 'cottage' as a gentleman's residence, designed by an architect, not really a natural cottage, to be lived in as a cottage, at all. Mrs Dashwood and her daughters, forced to leave their own house when Mr Dashwood dies and their half-brother inherits, move into such a cottage, clearly much more commodious than the minimum just described, though seeming small to those who have just moved out of Norland. This is an example of the new variety—almost a development from the dower house—built to be the home of tenants and dependants and such women of private, though limited, means as Mrs Dashwood is. At a very much higher level is the obviously prosperous, comfortable, pretty and modern cottage at Uppercross in *Persuasion*, 'elevated from a farm-house' for the squire's son on his marriage, and lived in by him, his wife, two children, a nurserymaid, and several other servants:

Uppercross Cottage, with its viranda [sic], French windows, and other prettinesses, was quite as likely to catch the traveller's eye, as the more consistent and considerable aspect and premises of the Great House, about a quarter of a mile farther on.

(*P*, 5)

It represents a change from the older tradition which would have absorbed Charles's family into the parental one at the hall.

A farmhouse, with outbuildings and farmyard discreetly behind it.

The farmhouse is more considerable, designed for more than merely living in, and for more than a single family. It varies considerably from one part of the country to another, and according to the prosperity of the region and the individual farmer, whether tenant or freehold. Generally a farmer employed labour, so some farm-hands—bachelors or unmarried girls—lived with the family. The house therefore has attic bedrooms and a large kitchen, as well as a family dining-room, and a parlour. Living and working space is intermingled and kept compact, sensibly, if not, by modern standards, hygienically. Whatever is women's business is all in one place, usually near the kitchen: the scullery and the dairy, and the brew-house and bake-house if these exist separate from the kitchen. Farmhouses of course have outbuildings which, as may still be seen, are added where convenient: barns, byres, and stables appear as circumstances require and money permits. Farm-buildings are unsightly, and one of Crawford's demands for Edmund's future home, the parsonage at Thornton Lacey, is that the farmyard shall be cleared away. It is a measure of young Robert Martin's prosperity, in *Emma*, that his house has a 'broad, neat gravel-walk, which led between espalier apple-trees to the front door' (*E*, 23) — evidently a very respectable entrance.

A farm is often attached to the house and land of those who are more than farmers. The Collinses in *Pride and Prejudice* keep pigs (there is such a fuss when Miss De Bourgh calls that Elizabeth thinks they must have got into the garden); and at a higher level is the gentleman-farmer like Elizabeth's father Mr Bennet, who lives the life of a gentleman, in a gentleman's house, whose wife has nothing to do with farm management and who, though he knows when his daughter cannot have any of the horses because they are wanted on the farm, plainly has all the work on it done by proxy, and is himself free to work, or idle, in his library for most of the day. Most gentlemen's houses have farms attached, although they are plainly not themselves to be classed as farmhouses, and as far as possible the farm buildings are concealed or removed to a distance, so as not to mar the architectural effect of the residence.

Both cottages and farms belong to the village, the centre of the community to which their occupants belong, however removed the individual dwelling may be. The village contains the elements which make up society: the church, the inn, and whatever crafts-men and tradesmen are required. In her picture of village life, or rather the one she presumes her readers possess while reading her novels, Jane Austen is rather old-fashioned. The life she draws on, which she herself knew, is rooted in the eighteenth century. It does not draw at all upon the Industrial Revolution, whose effects were felt first in the Midlands and the North, where villages grew rapidly into manufacturing towns, which, looking inwards to the factories which supplied work for their inhabitants, soon became quite separate from the life of the countryside around them. Jane Austen's own Hampshire was then, and is still, a farming county, its county town of Winchester having even now virtually no industry, nor having grown much from its early nineteenth-century self. The villages of the novels, whether in Devon, Somerset, Hertfordshire, Northamptonshire, or Surrey, are all of the same kind: a community to a large extent self-sufficient, making a large part of its own requirements in tools, furnishings, and clothing, as well as its own corn, meat, and beer. The pros-perous may send, or procure, from the larger town or from London the desiderata of comfortable living; Jane Austen invites the reader to notice the extent to which her characters do so: to note General Tilney and his Staffordshire china, or Frank Churchill ordering a piano from London, or, the height of nonsensical extravagance (the pretext which enables him to order the piano), getting his hair cut.

One sign of the times, and of general prosperity, is the village shop in *Emma*, which contradicts the ominous warnings sounded by Miss Bates's uncertain future, Jane Fairfax's fate as a governess, and the ostler at the Crown asking for parish relief. The completely self-sufficing community has plainly disappeared, and the delightful picture we receive of what is now a long-past way of life was, when Jane Austen wrote, a picture of something new. The shop is a link with the industrial world, where can be found 'a charming collection of new ribbons from town' (*E*, 27), from London, that is, but ultimately from their place of manufacture; where Harriet can have her choice of muslins, possibly from India; and where Frank Churchill can buy gloves, from 'sleek well-tied parcels of "Men's Beavers" and "York Tan"' (*E*, 24) the latters' name revealing their origin far from Highbury.

Highbury itself receives one charming vignette, viewed from the doorway of this same shop:

> Much could not be hoped from the traffic of even the busiest part of Highbury:—Mr Perry walking hastily by, Mr William Cox letting himself in at his office door, Mr Cole's carriage horses returning from exercise, or a stray letter-boy on an obstinate mule, were the liveliest objects she could presume to expect; and when her eyes fell only on the butcher with his tray, a tidy old woman travelling homewards from shop with her full basket, two curs quarrelling over a dirty bone, and a string of dawdling children round the baker's little bow-window eyeing the ginger bread, she knew she had no reason to complain, and was amused enough.
>
> (*E*, 27)

Highbury, like all other places of its size, and even less, has its inn—the Crown, its secular centre, just as the parish church is its spiritual one. The inn serves a number of useful functions. It is primarily the place at which travellers may stay overnight on journeys; it is, if on a recognised route, the point at which horses drawing public and mail coaches are kept, changed, and rested; it will also keep horses of its own which may be hired by those

'The King's Arms, Dorchester', by Thomas Rowlandson.

travelling 'post', who will use them on the next 'stage', to the next inn, change them again there, and leave them to be brought back when they convey another traveller in the reverse direction. Horses are hired also to local people who have a carriage, but do not go to the expense of keeping horses of their own: people like the fashionable Hursts in *Pride and Prejudice* who cannot afford to, or like Mr Knightley in *Emma*, who, 'having little spare money and a great deal of health, activity, and independence, was too apt, in Emma's opinion, to get about as he could, and not use the carriage so often as became the owner of Donwell Abbey' (*E*, 26). The inn is also, then as now, whether a coaching inn or not, a social centre. Jane Austen, unlike a later woman writer, George Eliot, does not concern herself with what goes on in the public bar or tap-room, but her inn, the Crown, serves the gentry as well as the labourers, as the newcomer Frank Churchill's first view of it reveals:

> Their first pause was at the Crown Inn, an inconsiderable place, though the principal one of the sort, where a couple of pair of post-horses were kept, more for the convenience of the neighbourhood than from any run on the road; and his companions had not

expected to be detained by any interest excited there; but in passing it they gave the history of the large room visibly added; it had been built many years ago for a ball-room, and while the neighbourhood had been in a particularly populous, dancing state, had been occasionally used as such;—but such brilliant days had long passed away, and now the highest purpose for which it was ever wanted was to accommodate a whist club established among the gentlemen and half-gentlemen of the place.

(E, 24)

The Crown is thus the small-town equivalent of the assembly rooms of a larger place; one of the novel's finest episodes is its recall to life as such, when a ball actually takes place.

The most important dwellings—what Jane Austen would term the most considerable—are the house of the local landowner, and other gentlemen's residences. While the size of a house is decided by income, its shape is decided by the kind of life for which it is designed. Jane Austen's is the period when domestic building in England was probably at its best, not only for fitness to its purpose,[1] but architecturally and aesthetically, as is proved by how desirable houses of the period still are today. Jane Austen writes of the class whose habits and houses have been the most lasting, and are still the most familiar. Rooms sound familiar, and have familiar uses; her most frequented indoor scenes are the drawing-room and the dining-room. When, as often, she does not tell the reader where a conversation takes place, the reader still feels confident (as Jane Austen intended he should) in imagining its setting. In her six major novels, she rarely sets a scene in a house which has not the usual rooms, or the usual number of them. The only two important exceptions are people who live in lodgings. The Bates in *Emma* have only part of a house, with one living-room, 'a very moderate sized apartment, which was everything to them' (*E*, 19); and Mrs Smith, Anne's invalid friend in *Persuasion*, is even worse off: 'her accommodations were limited to a noisy parlour, and a dark

---

[1] For the purposes of those for whom it was designed that is; servants' convenience and comforts were not always so much considered; but even here more thought is given to their needs than fifty years later, when some Victorian town houses show a horrifying carelessness as to how menials lived and worked.

The Saloon, Saltram House, Devon.

bedroom behind' (*P*, 17). At the upper end of the scale are the splendid mansions, like Mr Rushworth's Sotherton in *Mansfield Park*, which has even its own chapel, or Lady Catherine's Rosings in *Pride and Prejudice*, whose grandeur is revealed in its having a small summer breakfast parlour—implying several larger rooms for other seasons, and for other meals—and having a piano even in the housekeeper's room. In between come houses with other suggestions of grandeur, comfort, or convenience; Cleveland, in *Sense and Sensibility*, has a billiard room for Mr Palmer to waste time in; both Mr Bennet and Mr Darcy in *Pride and Prejudice* have a library, though with considerable differences in scale; and Mansfield Park has a schoolroom and nursery.

Jane Austen is always clear in her own mind as to the size and shape of the various houses she invents, but descends to few details, because her houses are not generally at all out of the ordinary: Northanger Abbey, the most unusual, is the one of which most details are given. The best rooms in a Georgian or Regency house are the living-rooms, which are often, as is common in many houses up to the twentieth century, upstairs. The situation of the whole of Miss Bates's dwelling, above a shop, is said to be 'on the drawing-room floor' (*E*, 19); while the Gardiner children, in *Pride and Prejudice*, coming half-way down the stairs to meet their cousins Jane and Elizabeth, have just left some of the main rooms, whether living-room or school-room. Even modest houses, like grand ones, have rather two 'fronts' than a front and a back, kitchens and offices being thrust to the side. Situation and lighting of rooms is thought of; Elizabeth wonders why Charlotte, at Hunsford, has chosen the room she has, when the dining parlour 'was a better sized room, and had a pleasanter aspect' (*PP*, 30), then realises that the inconvenience has advantages: 'Mr Collins would undoubtedly have been much less in his own apartment [his study], had they sat in one equally lively' (*ibid.*). Sunshine in a living-room is to be avoided, partly no doubt because it faded furnishings, as well as tanning skins; Lady Catherine sums up the Bennet's arrangements:

> 'This must be a most inconvenient sitting room for the evening, in summer; the windows are full west.'
>
> (*PP*, 56)

Servants' working quarters are kept out of sight: Catherine contrasts 'the few shapeless pantries and a comfortless scullery' (*NA*, 23) at Fullerton with the range of rooms at Northanger Abbey, impressively containing 'every modern invention to facilitate the labour of the cooks', but deplorable to Catherine because they take up the oldest part of what had been the convent. Servants sleep in attics; it is a measure of Fanny Price's humble status at Mansfield that she also sleeps on the top storey, where the attics are.

The country house, and the life which it entails, are a particularly English and particularly eighteenth-century phenomenon, which organised the lives of a good part of the population. Most of the development of eighteenth-century culture, which is all within its shadow, had gone into it by the time Jane Austen was writing.

The house and estate provide work and keep for most of the people who live there. The impression Jane Austen is sometimes accused of giving, of a life where men do no work and no-one exists below the rank of gentlemen, is one she could not have suggested to a contemporary. They would know as she did that the squire who ran his household and estate had a real and valuable job, and note when such men in her novels fail in their duties: like Mr Palmer playing billiards, or Sir Walter Elliot overspending, and surrendering his responsibilities to an agent, and finally to a tenant. She expects her reader to notice also when a man is performing his duties: like Mr Darcy considering it only proper to build up his library, and Mr Knightley attending to his affairs, in conference with William Larkins. Though these men have a civilised amount of leisure, and the responsibility for using their time profitably is their own, they are very far from being idle rich. As employers of large numbers of people, both in the house and garden and on the estate, and as landlords of a varying number of tenants, they have a powerful and far-reaching influence on their community.

Their wives, or those who assume for them the responsibilities of the woman of the house, also have their influence. What these duties are (already discussed in Chapter 3) and how they perform them, is, for Jane Austen, always a test of character. Although we never hear of Emma's dealings with the housekeeper, butler, cook, and various maids, personal and household, through them she creates a house that runs smoothly enough to content the habits and tastes of her nervous father, and yet can cope without strain with a visit from her unaccompanied infant nephews and nieces. A woman is responsible also for the welfare of employees and tenants. The reproach Emma takes most to heart is Mr Knightley's, that she has been ungenerous to Miss Bates; and we have very much earlier been told of one of her great virtues, that she

was very compassionate; and the distresses of the poor were as sure of relief from her patience, as from her purse. She understood their ways, could allow for their ignorance and their temptations, had no romantic expectations of extraordinary virtue from those, for whom education had done so little; entered into their troubles with ready sympathy, and always gave her assistance with as much intelligence as good-will.

(E, 10)

The foundation of the middle-class way of life is the resident servant—a fact Jane Austen makes it easy to overlook, since she rarely mentions servants, and never makes them into even minor characters. There are nevertheless many signs of their existence. Characters refer to them casually, by name, as to someone with a place in the scheme of things so well known as not to need mentioning. Jane Austen, however, expects her reader to register that when Mr Bingley refers to Nicholls he means his housekeeper, that the Searle who so well understands the boiling of an egg is Mr Woodhouse's cook, and that the relative position of lady's maids, housemaids, and dependent relatives has been perfectly caught when Lady Bertram on a memorable occasion sends her own maid to Fanny:

> It had really occurred to her that Fanny, preparing for a ball, might be glad of better help than the upper house-maid's, and when dressed herself, she actually sent her own maid to assist her; too late of course to be of any use. Mrs Chapman had just reached the attic floor, when Miss Price came out of her room completely dressed, and only civilities were necessary—but Fanny felt her aunt's attention almost as much as Lady Bertram or Mrs Chapman could do themselves.
>
> (MP, 28)

It is normal for a lady to have a maid to help her dress, so Jane Austen does not feel called upon to mention the fact, except where the lack is significant, as here, or incidental, as when Emma, returned home after Mr Elton has so wildly proposed to her, has to wait to be alone; 'the hair was curled, and the maid sent away, and Emma sat down to think and be miserable' (E, 16).

A servant is a necessity of comfortable living—a fact not so shocking or surprising when the circumstances of the time are taken into account. Service is practically the only employment open to girls in the country, whose own families' resources are inadequate to keep them, where they cannot take any of the dubious openings such as a city affords, like factories or shops, and who do not themselves possess enough learning to be able to teach. There is no doubt that where there is no check on employers, servants can be wickedly overworked, underpaid, and underfed. There is equally no doubt that a good 'place' can be a good thing, providing a living, some training in huswifery, and an ordered existence where each member serves a useful purpose, and enjoys possibly more comfort and a higher standard of living than in the home from which the servant has come. One constantly gains the impression, in reading Jane Austen, that the servants, little though she alludes to them, are individuals, and recognised as such. One suspects that not only is Miss Bates wise to stretch her small income into employing a maid of all work, but that it may well be for the comfort of the maid as well. Her name, Patty, is always used in referring to her; the reader notices the contrast when Mrs Elton refers to 'one of our men, I forgot his name' (*E*, 34): the remark is meant as a boast, but shows her to be inconsiderate. Mr Woodhouse also considers the convenience and personalities of his servants, self-centred and comically inadequate though he is: his coachman, James, for instance, he says, 'will not like to put the horses to for such a little way' (*E*, 1) as the half mile to Randalls, and James's daughter Hannah, housemaid at Randalls, has his approval, as a 'civil, pretty-spoken girl . . . I observe she always turns the lock of the door the right way, and never bangs it' (*ibid.*).

When it is to Jane Austen's purpose to give full details of an establishment, she can be explicit. Miss Bates, as already mentioned, has only Patty to look after them, as the reader is told because the Bates's straitened circumstances are an important element in the novel. The only other households which we know in full are in the most money-ridden novel, *Sense and Sensibility*. Mrs Dashwood's cottage, with four bedrooms and two garrets, holds herself, her three daughters, two maids, and a man servant, whom she maintains on £500 a year. Jane Austen makes it clear that this is practicable though not opulent; but that to keep a horse (which Willoughby offers to Marianne) and the groom required to look after it, is out of the question. Mrs Jennings, ever practical, later in the novel sums up the prospects for Edward

Ferrars, if, when he marries Lucy, his mother gives him £500 a year:

> 'How snug they might live in such another cottage as yours—or a little bigger—with two maids and two men; and I believe I could help them to a housemaid, for my Betty has a sister out of place, that would fit them exactly.'

Then, on learning that Edward's family has cast him off:

> 'Wait for his living!—aye, we all know how *that* will end;—they will wait a twelve month, and finding no good comes of it, they will set down upon a curacy of fifty pounds a year, with the interest of his two thousand pounds, and what little matter Mr Steele and Mr Pratt can give her . . . Two maids and two men, indeed! . . . No, no, they must get a stout girl of all works—Betty's sister would never do for them *now*.'
>
> (SS, 37)

No critics of her day quibbled at Jane Austen's economics, which to mention at all shows assurance of their truth. Such quotations make clear that different kinds of servants are almost in different trades: Betty's sister is no 'stout girl of all works', any more than Lady Bertram's personal maid Chapman is to be equated with the upper house-maid. It is part of the mistress's duty to get and train her staff; the most dreadful indictment of the bad mistress and the bad servant is the small details of the state of things in the Price household at Portsmouth:

> the tea-board never thoroughly cleaned, the cups and saucers wiped in streaks, the milk a mixture of motes floating in thin blue, and the bread and butter growing every minute more greasy than even Rebecca's hands had first produced it.
>
> (MP, 46)

the few small details stands for all the consequences of a woman who was

> wishing to be an economist, without contrivance or regularity; dissatisfied with her servants, without skill to make them better, and whether helping, or reprimanding, or indulging them, without any power of engaging their respect.
>
> (MP, 39)

CHAPTER SEVEN

The Busy Hum of Men

JUST as the farm and the cottage look to the village, so the village in its turn looks to the local town, and beyond it lie the larger county towns, and beyond all, the centre of the fashionable world, almost a world in itself, London. The country is rapidly becoming more coherent in Jane Austen's time, mainly as a result of better communications and faster travel. The means of getting about are greatly improved, both for goods and for people. The beginning of the improvement is better roads. Where formerly the upkeep of roads had been the duty of individual parishes it has now become the responsibility of turnpike companies. They are given parliamentary powers to erect gates and toll bars, whereby the fees of the road-users themselves pay for the upkeep of the roads—a much fairer system, and a much more effective one. Minor roads may remain bad, and be fit for horseback travel only, but the main roads are now good enough to encourage the building and owning of light, fast carriages. How fast travel, under the best conditions, can actually be, is revealed by Mr Darcy, talking to Elizabeth about the distance between Charlotte, married to Mr Collins and living in Kent, and her parents in Hertfordshire:

'What is fifty miles of good road? Little more than half a day's journey. Yes, I call it a *very* easy distance.'

(*PP*, 33)

The boasting Mrs Elton gives another instance:

'What is distance, Mr Weston, to people of large fortune?—You would be amazed to hear how my brother, Mr Suckling, sometimes flies about. You will hardly believe me—but twice in one week he and Mr Bragge went to London and back again with four horses.'

(*E*, 36)

The West Country Mails at the Gloucester Coffee House, Piccadilly.

that is, five hundred miles altogether, according to the distances Mrs Elton gives from Maple Grove to London.

Carriages are still uncomfortable by modern standards, and long journeys are very tiring, and cramped. The Miss Dashwoods in *Sense and Sensibility*, travelling from Barton in Devonshire to London 'reached town by three o'clock the third day'. Other trials are decreasing. Jane Austen plainly considers highway robbery a thing of the past, to be mentioned only to be ridiculed; when Catherine Moreland is on her way to Bath she says ironically

> 'neither robbers nor tempests befriended them, nor one lucky over-turn to introduce them to the hero.'

> (*NA*, 2)

On the other hand, Byron considers robbers on Shooters Hill (outside London) a probable hazard for his hero Don Juan in Canto XI of that poem, published in 1823; and one of Jane Austen's

closest friends was killed in a carriage accident. Journeys, however, at what is the beginning of the great age of coach travel,
which ceased only with the institution of railways, increase: for
visits, to town for the season, to Bath, Scarborough, and to all the
other watering places like Wales, the English Lakes, and the
Highlands of Scotland.

There are many different kinds of carriages. The lowest,
socially, is the public vehicle, the stage-coach, not considered
suitable for ladies of the class of which Jane Austen writes, or to
which she belongs. Her letters abound with discussion of arrangements whereby various members of the family can be conveyed in
private vehicles belonging to other members of the family.

Many different types of family and private carriage are mentioned, whose names are so alike as to sound almost synonymous.
However, the differences can occasionally be important. The usual
family vehicle is a chaise, which holds three people, like the one in

A curricle-hung gig.

which Fanny, Edmund, and Fanny's sister Susan return from Portsmouth to Mansfield. Very similar to it are the two other four-wheeled vehicles, the coach (which can hold six people) and the chariot. Smart young men have smart fast vehicles, like John Thorpe's curricle-hung gig, while the most memorable vehicle of all in the novels, Mrs Elton's sister's barouche-landau, is plainly a status symbol, which was announced in the *Morning Post* for 5 January 1804 in uncomplimentary terms:

> Mr Buxton, the celebrated whip, has just launched a new-fangled machine, a kind of *nondescript*. It is described by the inventor to be the due medium between a landau and a barouche, but all who have seen it say it more resembles a fish-cart or a music-caravan.[1]

There are gradations to be observed in the novels between those who, like General Tilney, own both the fashionable chaise and four, the horses to put to it, and the outriders to accompany it; those who, like Mr Bennet, use the same horses for the carriage and for farm-work; and those who, like Mr Bingley's sister and brother-in-law, having a carriage, but no horses, depend upon hiring or borrowing.

Even though people were becoming more mobile, society was

[1] As quoted in R. W. Chapman's edition of *Mansfield Park*, Oxford, 1934.

still local. Many families, like Jane Austen's in her youth, depended happily on what the neighbourhood could offer. In her early years Jane Austen lived at Steventon, a small village (almost as isolated now as it was then) which looked to Basingstoke as its market town, as its nearest and appropriate centre for trade, and for the wider and more public kind of social life that involved more than the immediate local families. In the last years of her life, after time spent at Bath and Southampton, she lived at Chawton, also in Hampshire, not far by modern standards from where she was born. But Chawton is aligned with Alton, barely two miles off—it is now almost joined—and in the other direction with the county town, Winchester, an assize town, a cathedral city, and a place of even more importance then than now. Jane Austen's letters contain accounts of visits to Winchester, and shopping errands to be performed there, as well as visits to be made. John Keats, who stayed there in 1819, bursts into some vivid and entertaining morsels of observation in his letters:

> The whole town is beautifully wooded—From the Hill at the Eastern extremity you see a prospect of Streets, and old Buildings mixed up with the trees. Then there are the most beautiful streams about I ever saw—full of Trout.
> The side streets here are excessively maiden-lady like: the door-steps always fresh from the flannel. The knockers have a staid, serious, nay almost awful quietness about them.—I never saw so quiet a collection of Lions' and Rams' heads.
> There is a fine Cathedral, a College, a Roman Catholic Chapel, a Methodist do., an independent do.,—and there is not one loom or any thing like manufacturing beyond bread and butter in the whole city.[1]

Jane Austen also visited London, where her brother Henry lived, and thence sent news of visits to shops, to exhibitions, to concerts, and the theatre—as well as to the dentist's. The rapid improvements of the time in the condition of roads encouraged such travel to the towns, so that villages no longer needed to be self-subsisting, and village trades declined, and towns enlarged, as a consequence. As Jane Austen's unambitious and unassuming life is regulated, so is that of many others of her time, and that of many characters

---

[1] Letters to Fanny Keats, Saturday 28 August, to John Hamilton Reynolds, Tuesday 21 September, to George and Georgiana Keats, Friday 17–Monday 27 September 1819.

in her novels, with different emphases determined by distance, wealth, and other outside circumstances. Although none of the novels is set in a town (though parts of *Northanger Abbey* and *Persuasion* take place in Bath, and a large part of *Sense and Sensibility* in London), the influence of the local town is often seen, and the greater pull of the more remote, like the watering-place and seaside resort, or the metropolis London itself, is felt.

The towns Jane Austen uses are a mixture of the imaginary and the actual. She does not hesitate to set events in London, in the famous watering-place, Bath, the popular seaside resorts of Brighton and Lyme Regis, or the naval town of Portsmouth; while alongside these she invents the Meryton and Lambton of *Pride and Prejudice*, which thus rank themselves more with the invented villages which occur in all the novels.

In general one might say that Jane Austen sets her novels in the country, with excursions to the city, and that the small nearby town plays little part in her literary scheme. Consequently the local government of the country, which she must have known well, knowing those who administered it, forms no part of her material. Local law is provided by Justices of the Peace, who decide the amount of the local rate and the spending of it. They are appointed nominally by the crown, but actually by the Lord Lieutenant, who is in his turn influenced by the local gentry. J.P.'s administer justice in Quarter or Petty sessions, or in private houses. They also operate the poor rate and poor relief, and see to the upkeep of roads, prisons, and work-houses; but as they have no official staff, and frequently not much money to work with, such services are haphazard.

There is no police force in England until Peel's blue-coats in 1829. The lack is not very serious in well-populated rural districts such as Jane Austen writes of, with their efficient 'neighbourhood of voluntary spies' which, Henry Tilney assures Catherine, keeps society safe from murderous husbands. The settled state of England in general says much for the eighteenth-century assumption that law and order is natural, and will prevail. Yet people lived with the fear of rebellion, as they must with the French Revolution so close both in distance and in time. In large towns, especially London, where the disorderly could congregate and co-operate, there was danger from sudden crime and violence. Against such a background Harriet's fright from the gipseys in *Emma*, from whom she is rescued with such address by Frank Churchill, becomes not quite so trivial as it seems, for there is no village policeman to aid her. That other nervous subject, Mr Woodhouse, for whom robbing a hen-roost is equivalent to house-breaking, ridiculous though he is, knows that, in a case of real house-breaking, he has no-one but himself, Emma, and his servants to depend upon, even though the local magistrate is Mr Knightley, and no redress but the doubtful and distant one of the local assizes at Kingston.

Such allusions as those to Kingston show Jane Austen aware of the relevance of town to country life, even in those novels not set in towns. Kingston is the nearest and most convenient place for Mr Knightley to go (on what one presumes is agricultural business) where he is willing to do errands for Miss Bates; in *Persuasion* Mrs Musgrove mentions that her husband 'always attends the assizes' (*P*, 8) which, in Somerset, would be at Taunton; while Northampton, Mansfield's nearest town, is somewhat inaccessible, when Mary wishes to have her harp brought thence. The one novel in which the country town figures largely is *Pride and Prejudice*, where the Bennet girls are within walking distance of Meryton, which offers all the pleasures of shops and shop-windows. Its size is suggested by its being big enough to absorb into billets a regiment of the militia.

All towns are smaller by far at the opening of the nineteenth century than now, and felt their links with the surrounding country very much more powerfully. A delightful recreation of the atmosphere of a past age, which is apt, although a quarter of a century later than Jane Austen, is Thomas Hardy's of the Dorchester of the 1840's, which he revives as the Casterbridge of *The Mayor of Casterbridge*:

> [It] was a place deposited in the block upon a corn-field. There was no suburb in the modern sense, or transitional intermixture of town and down. It stood, with regard to the wide fertile land adjoining, clean-cut and distinct, like a chess-board on a green table-cloth. The farmer's boy could sit under his barley-mow and pitch a stone into the office-window of the town clerk; reapers at work among the sheaves nodded to acquaintances standing on the pavement corner; the red-robed judge, when he condemned a sheep-stealer,

pronounced sentence to the tune of Baa, that floated in at the window from the remainder of the flock hard by; and at executions the waiting crowd stood in a meadow immediately before the drop, out of which the cows had been temporarily driven to give the spectators room.

(*The Mayor of Casterbridge*, Chapter 14)

Jane Austen makes more use of the kind of town that is less in harmony and union with the surrounding country, such as has another reason for existence, besides that of being a market or a centre for the execution of justice. The spa, to which people travel for medical reasons, in order to take a course of the supposedly beneficial mineral waters which are its claim to fame, was a well-established feature of eighteenth-century life. The seaside resort, to which people go for the supposed benefits to health of sea-bathing, comes rather later. Both feature largely in the life and amusements of Jane Austen's time and in her novels. Her only spa is Bath (unless one counts the brief mention of Bakewell in Derbyshire, in *Pride and Prejudice*), which she herself visited and where she lived for four years, from 1801 to 1805, and which appears, in two very different aspects, in *Northanger Abbey* and in *Persuasion*. Several seaside places are mentioned: Dawlish in *Sense and Sensibility*, where the fool and fop Robert Ferrars goes with his smart and cunning bride Lucy Steele; the famous Brighton in *Pride and Prejudice*, scene of Lydia Bennet's downfall; Weymouth, in *Emma*, where Frank Churchill met Jane Fairfax; and Lyme Regis in *Persuasion*, where Anne Elliot sees a second spring in her life begin to dawn for her.

The city of Bath was mostly built between 1760 and 1810, and so was in its full bloom both of fashion and beauty when Jane Austen saw it. Originally famed for medical reasons, for the chemical springs which were known even in Roman times, it rose suddenly to fashion the eighteenth century. With an increase of wealth which enabled more people to share in a fashionable life, a growing ease of travel caused by improved roads and coaches, and by a more prosperous and law-abiding country, Bath became an alternative to London as a place to spend the 'season', full of amusements for the young, as well as agreeable modes of taking a cure for the middle-aged and elderly. It is a less expensive place than London at which to live the fashionable life: for this reason

Jane Austen's Bath. *Above* The Upper Rooms, and *below* the Lower Rooms.

Mr Shepherd in *Persuasion* feels relieved when his extravagant employer Sir Walter Elliot decides to live there, rather than in London, when he has been forced to let Kellynch Hall. It is also a place to which one may retire, as Mrs Rushworth, in *Mansfield Park*, put in the position of a 'dowager' when her son marries Maria Bertram,

> very early in November removed herself, her maid, her footman, and her chariot, with true dowager propriety.
>
> (*MP*, 21)

The young Jane Austen of *Northanger Abbey* (written in 1798) sees Bath as the delightful scene of the delightful young heroine Catherine Morland's adventures. It is a place whose conduct has been established by the two famous 'beaux', Nash and Brummel, where people did set things at fixed times. The *Historic and Local New Bath Guide* for 1802 explains that

> there are two Dress Balls every week, viz. on Monday at the New Rooms [that is the Upper Rooms], and on Friday at the Lower Rooms. . . . There are also two Fancy Balls every week, viz. at the Lower Rooms on Tuesday, and at the New Rooms on Thursday . . . and nine Subscription Concerts, and three Choral Nights, in the winter at the New Rooms, on Wednesday, under the direction of Mr Rauzzini.[1]

while at the Theatre 'the days of performance are, in general, Tuesdays, Thursdays, and Saturdays'. Henry Tilney, that delightful commentator throughout *Northanger Abbey*, sums up Bath with amused irony:

> 'Bath, compared with London, has little variety, and so everybody finds out every year. "For six weeks, I allow Bath is pleasant enough; but beyond *that*, it is the most tiresome place in the world." You would be told so by people of all descriptions, who come regularly every winter, lengthen the six weeks into ten or twelve, and go away when they can afford to stay no longer.'
>
> (*NA*, 10)

The Jane Austen of *Persuasion*, written within a year of her death in 1817, finds less to please her gentle, less happy, and less vigorous heroine Anne Elliot, who dreaded 'the possible heats of September in all the white glare of Bath' (*P*, 5); her eventual arrival there

---

[1] As quoted by R. W. Chapman, *Northanger Abbey* and *Persuasion*, Oxford, 1933.

produces a vivid little scene, which, though dwelling upon noise and discomfort, has a nostalgic charm:

> When Lady Russell ... was entering Bath on a wet afternoon, and driving through the long course of streets from the Old Bridge to Camden-place, amidst the dash of other carriages, the heavy rumble of carts and drays, the bawling of newsmen, muffin men and milk-men and the ceaseless clink of pattens, she made no complaint. No, these were noises which belonged to the winter pleasures; her spirits rose under their influence, and ... she was feeling, though not saying, that, after being so long in the country, nothing could be so good for her as a little quiet cheerfulness.
>
> (P, 2)

The cult of the seaside is a more recent and different though allied one. George III paid his first visit to Weymouth in 1789, and by patronising it gave impetus to the fashion. Going to the sea began with the quest for health, and the belief that sea-bathing was a remedy for all sorts of complaints.

It began with the rise of Scarborough, already a spa, as a place where sea-bathing also was medically beneficial. In 1702 Sir John Floyer and Edward Baynard, two London medical men, published a volume extolling the sea as the cure for almost any chronic complaint—asthma, cancer, consumption, deafness, ruptures, rheumatism, and madness. Scarborough was an established bathing resort by the 1730's (Sheridan, revising Vanbrugh's play *The Relapse* in 1781, called it *A Trip to Scarborough*), and became a pattern for later towns, with its Assembly Rooms, Circulating Library, and Theatre. In 1796 Burns's doctor recommended sea-bathing in the Solway for the dying poet; while Mrs Bennet in *Pride and Prejudice* prescribes it for her own nerves, confident that 'a little sea-bathing would set [her] up for ever' (*PP*, 41). Bathing was a serious business, to be undertaken under medical supervision, with formality and attention to decorum. One hired a bathing-machine, in which one could disrobe privately, which was pulled into the water by a horse, and from which one could descend into the water under cover of a hood—all in strict seclusion.

Bathing was no mere matter of pleasure. It was at first a matter for the winter months, and for the very early morning, and so something of an ordeal even on the south coast, but still more of

one in the windy north-east at Scarborough. However, anything,
even medical treatment, that entails leaving home, may be turned
into a holiday; sea-bathing places rapidly turned into places of
pleasure, as spas had done before them. They were assisted in
so doing by the growing enthusiasm for the picturesque in nature,
which led to the visiting of wild or romantic scenery. Since the
sea-coast is often both, popular places were often also pretty
ones. George III favoured, as well as Weymouth, Lyme Regis,
about which Jane Austen commits herself to one of her rare bursts
of delight:

> a very strange stranger it must be, who does not see charms in the
> immediate environs of Lyme, to make him wish to know it better.
> The scenes in its neighbourhood, Charmouth, with its high grounds
> and extensive sweeps of country, and still more its sweet retired
> bay, backed by dark cliffs, where fragments of low rock among the
> sands make it the happiest spot for watching the flow of the tide, for
> sitting in unwearied contemplation;—the woody varieties of the
> cheerful village of Up Lyme, and, above all, Pinny, with its green
> chasms between romantic rocks, where the scattered forest trees
> and orchards of luxuriant growth declare that many a generation
> must have passed away since the first partial falling of the cliff
> prepared the ground for such a state, where a scene so wonderful
> and so lovely is exhibited, as may more than equal any of the
> resembling scenes of the far-famed Isle of Wight: these places must
> be visited, and visited again, to make the worth of Lyme understood.

An entertaining and equally uncharacteristic outburst comes
from Coleridge: *On Revisiting the Sea-Shore; after long absence, under
strong medical recommendation not to bathe*, which had had as an earlier
title *A flowering weed on the sweet Hill of Poesy*:

> God be with thee, gladsome Ocean!
>   How gladly greet I thee once more!
> Ships and waves, and ceaseless motion,
>   And men rejoicing on thy shore.
> Dissuading spake the mild Physician,
>   'Those briny waves for thee are Death!'
> But my soul fulfilled her mission,
>   And lo! I breathe untroubled breath!
>
> Fashion's pining sons and daughters,
>   That seek the crowd they seem to fly,

Trembling they approach thy waters;
　And what cares Nature, if they die?

Me a thousand hopes and pleasures,
　A thousand recollections bland,
Thoughts sublime, and stately measures,
　Revisit on thy echoing strand:

Dreams (the Soul herself forsaking),
　Tearful raptures, boyish mirth;
Silent adorations, making
　A blessed shadow of this Earth!

O ye hopes, that stir within me,
　Health comes with you from above!
God is with me, God is in me!
　I cannot die, if Life be Love.

While a number of seaside places become frequented and prosperous at this time, undoubtedly the best known and most successful one, sought by rich and poor, is Brighton, formerly the little fishing village of Brighthelmstone, set in the South Downs, upon brilliant white cliffs, that became, mainly through the patronage of the Prince Regent, the favourite haunt of all London for the whole of the nineteenth century. Even before the coming of the railways, it was within convenient and easy reach of London, only 50 miles off. Cobbett, writing in 1821, remarks in his *Rural Rides* that stock-jobbers could live there '50 miles from the wen

The Steyne, at Regency Brighton.

The Royal Pavilion at Brighton.
Above The original Pavilion, by Henry Holland.
Below After its 'orientalisation' by Nash.

[meaning London] and carry on business there; it is situated so that a coach which leaves it not very early in the morning, reaches London by noon'. Where the Prince Regent went, went fashion. He spent a good deal of his time there, with his mistress Mrs Fitzherbert, going to vast expense to indulge his very various, and often estimable, tastes. For a considerable time unpopular with the London populace, particularly during the fierce disputes over his treatment of his wife (who behaved nearly as foolishly as he) he found in Brighton both refuge and opportunity. Though a luxurious *bon-vivant*, he was also a man of artistic taste and vigorous enthusiasm, who found an opportunity to exercise his talents in creating the Brighton Pavilion. This astonishing 'pleasure-dome' is in the heart of Brighton, an inspired blending of the wildly exotic and oriental, with the grace and proportion of the Neo-classical. The Prince, a connoisseur of contemporary *objets d'art*, particularly of French workmanship, furnished and equipped it in a style to match.

A feature of the watering-place is the library, from which Isabella Thorpe at Bath obtained the novels with astonishing titles which so alarmed and delighted Catherine Morland. Novels are the main supply of libraries, and supply primarily the wants of women. They are obtained by an annual subscription of up to one guinea for membership and a small payment of a penny for each volume borrowed. The customary method of publishing each novel in three volumes is thus very convenient for library circulation. Such books save Mary Musgrove, in *Persuasion*, from stagnation at Lyme Regis when, having insisted on staying instead of Anne to nurse Louisa after her accident, she finds time hanging heavy on her hands. More respectable volumes of a more serious nature—biography, essays, history, and poetry are mentioned—are borrowed by Fanny Price at Portsmouth for the double purpose of her own pleasure and her young sister Susan's neglected education. Such books were not always physically attractive, whatever their contents might be. At an earlier period than Jane Austen's, Sheridan's Lydia Languish laments:

Lydia: Did you enquire for *The Delicate Distress?*
Lucy: Or, *The Memoirs of Lady Woodford?* Yes, indeed, ma'am. I asked everywhere for it; and I might have brought it from

Mr Frederick's, but Lady Slattern Lounger, who had just sent it home, had so soiled and dog's-eared it, it wa'n't fit for a Christian to read.

Lydia: Heigh-ho! Yes, I always know when Lady Slattern has been before me. She has a most observing thumb; and, I believe, cherishes her nails for the convenience of making marginal notes.

(*The Rivals*, Act I, Scene 2)

At a later period, Mrs Gaskell's character Mrs Fitzpatrick, in *Wives and Daughters*, turns over the soiled pages with the scissors.

Libraries, as well as lenders of books, were shops; one at Brighton formed one of the pleasures of Lydia Bennet on her ill-fated visit where, she tells in her letters, 'such and such officer's attended them, and where she had seen such beautiful ornaments as made her quite wild' (*PP*, 42). Since they are places where patrons, in the nature of their business, have to loiter, they become places for casual meetings, for conversation, and society; it is an easy step to becoming places of assignation and dubious repute. Brighton bears witness to its own character in possessing two libraries. A local preacher in 1815, inveighing against 'The Temptations of Watering Places' finds idleness one of the greatest, and one to which the reading of 'every flimsy species of novels', and the places where they are procured, contribute. Such circumstances would all help to shock Mr Collins, in *Pride and Prejudice*, when, having offered to read, and been supplied with a book,

> on beholding it (for every thing announced it to be from a circulating library), he started back, and begging pardon, protested that he never read novels.
>
> (*PP*, 14)

As well as the attractions of fashion, Brighton offered more vulgarian temptations. Militia regiments were stationed there in 1793, 1794, and 1795, which became notorious, and which are almost certainly the ones on which Jane Austen was drawing when she invented Lydia Bennet's ill-fated visit, and Lydia's own ecstatic anticipations of it:

> In Lydia's imagination, a visit to Brighton comprised every possibility of earthly happiness. She saw with the creative eye of fancy, the streets of that gay bathing place covered with officers. She saw herself the object of attention, to tens and to scores of them at

The naval town of Portsmouth.

present unknown. She saw all the glories of the camp; its tents stretched forth in beauteous uniformity of lines, crowded with the young and the gay, and dazzling with scarlet; and to complete the view she saw herself seated beneath a tent, tenderly flirting with at least six officers at once.

(PP, 41)

Portsmouth, the place by the sea which is the setting for the final section of *Mansfield Park*, is not primarily either spa or resort. It is, as now, a naval station. Jane Austen herself was familiar with the life of those who are closely connected with the navy and the sea, and draws on her experiences in her account. The contrast between Portsmouth and Brighton reveals that Jane Austen is employing the nature of her setting, with which she expects her readers to be familiar, in order to emphasise what happens to her characters there: frivolity is natural to both Lydia and Brighton; struggling and hard-pressed naval families' lives are appropriate to Fanny Price, tormentedly suffering one of the greatest crises of her life.

London is of towns a *per se*, the capital of England, in many ways another world than the rest of the country, where, for Wordsworth,

> Ships, towers, domes, theatres and temples lie
> Open unto the fields, and to the sky;

Jane Austen's London, when Chelsea was still a village.

All bright and glittering in the smokeless air.
Never did sun more beautifully steep
In his first splendour valley, rock or hill;
Ne'er saw I, never felt, a calm so deep!
The river glideth at his own sweet will . . .[1]

another view is that of Byron's hero Don Juan, twenty years later:

A mighty mass of brick, and smoke, and shipping,
   Dirty and dusky, but as wide as eye
Could reach, with here and there a sail just skipping
   In sight, then lost amid the forestry
Of masts; a wilderness of steeples peeping
   On tip-toe through their sea-coal canopy;
A huge dun cupola, like a foolscap crown
On a fool's head—and there is London Town.[2]

London, the largest city by a long way (fifteen times larger than Bristol), which had doubled its population in the previous hundred years and was still rapidly increasing, was yet, with a population of 1,274,000 in 1820, not a large city by modern standards, and occupied only a comparatively small area—not much more than a tenth of its present sprawl. It comprised a number of boroughs which, while rapidly becoming joined together, still felt separate entities. The city proper was the chief and most powerful, both a port controlling the country's East India trade, as well as that with Europe, the Mediterranean, and Africa, a market to which all parts of the country came to buy and sell, and a manufacturing city employing the largest skilled labour to produce luxury goods— silk, china, and cabinet-making. Westminster, theoretically a separate city, and the seat of government and the court, is by Jane Austen's time inseparable, as residential districts spring up along the Strand and join the two. Although merchants still live at and over their places of business, a fashionable quarter is growing up round Covent Garden, Piccadilly, and Bloomsbury, peopled first by the aristocracy, then by the gentry who follow them, creating gradually the now famous London squares. Elegant though the new eighteenth-century London was and remains, it was a haphazard, arbitrary city, with no planned development like

---

[1] *Sonnet composed on Westminster Bridge, Sept.* 3, 1803.
[2] *Don Juan*, Canto X, lxxxii.

Edinburgh's New Town, built at the same period, mainly because, in expanding, it had to absorb already flourishing towns and villages.

Where people live is a sign of status. In *Sense and Sensibility* the John Dashwoods are very respectably situated in Harley Street; in *Pride and Prejudice* the Bingleys, equally so in Mr Hurst's house in Grosvenor Street, contrast with the Gardiners, who are in trade, and live, presumably close by it, in Gracechurch Street. Mary Crawford's fashionable friends, in *Mansfield Park*, live in Wimpole Street. Urban London soon gives way to country, and contemporary views show that there is still a heath worthy of the name at Hampstead, that Chelsea is still a village, and that the countryside still prevails at Clapham Common.

Although London had a huge resident population it had also a large temporary one, both of those who lived elsewhere and visited, and those who, while living and working in London, had also villas and country seats to which to retire and escape. It is the first of these that concern Jane Austen most closely, though one might instance the lawyer Mr John Knightley, Emma's brother-in-law, and his family, as an example of the second, who, though he does not own a country villa, retreats to visit Highbury, and takes holidays at Southend: he is an inhabitant of Brunswick Square, a sign of his prosperity.

Most of Jane Austen's characters who come to London do so merely for society, for the 'season'; in *Mansfield Park*, however, she touches upon one of the serious reasons for spending life half in the country and half in the town: that is, if one is the local Member of Parliament, as is Sir Thomas Bertram, whose wife is, however, too lethargic to accompany him. Sir Thomas occupies his seat (the party he belongs to is not mentioned) by virtue of his position as landowner; it is clear that his seat is never contested. Though he is both respectable and conscientious, many M.P.s were not. The electoral system of the period is notoriously inequitable, with boroughs whose bounds, fixed long since, now no longer bear much relation to the population of the country. Depopulated areas continue to send their representative, while the rapidly-growing population of the North of England is scarcely represented at all. Members, like Mr Palmer in *Sense and Sensibility*, got votes (given in public ballot and so open to pressure) by largesse, even bribery, and by all the more refined influence that landlord can wield over tenant or small-holder. The situation is farcically satirised by the novelist Thomas Love Peacock in *Melincourt*, in one episode of which Mr Oran Haut-ton (a very civilised flute-playing orang-outang, as his punning name suggests) stands as one of two candidates for the rotten borough of One-vote—and is elected. The situation is one that would have delighted Jane Austen, but one that, since politics are a masculine subject, she herself could not use.

On the whole, Jane Austen keeps to the class slightly below that of the parliamentary member. While it is true that there are undeniable class divisions in society, it is never easy to say decisively where one class gives way to the next above or below. Especially in London, the wealthy clergy and the cultivated middle-class intermingle with men of rank or power quite freely, if not on precisely equal terms. The examples of men who rise by merit are as conspicuous as those who are born to high places. Illustrious literary instances are Dr Johnson and Sir Walter Scott, while among men of action are Wolfe and Nelson. This mixture and flexibility are two things that preserved England from the revolution that France suffered, which was brought about, amongst other things, by the rigid separation of the aristocrats from the lower orders and the peasantry.

The way of life that goes with the possession of a town house is what chiefly affects London for the reader of Jane Austen's novels. She herself was familiar with London and paid a number of visits to her brother Henry and his wife Eliza, who lived in Sloane Street and later in Henrietta Street, Covent Garden, where he was a banker from 1807 to 1816. She does not attempt to suggest aristocratic and upper-class life, such as for a short period was embracing Lord Byron. Probably the most fashionable London occasions in her novels are the social engagements attended by Elinor and Marianne Dashwood, about which Jane Austen gives very few details. For the characters in Jane Austen's novels, as it must have been for many of their kind, London is a place for society, shopping, and amusements of all kinds. The society is a matter for the winter months, as the 'season' has always been: Elinor and Marianne Dashwood in *Sense and Sensibility* accompany

Wedgwood's shop in St James's Square.

Mrs Jennings thither at the beginning of January; Lydia, in London in August, and waiting in disgrace in Gracechurch Street for her wedding, laments that, 'to be sure London was rather thin, but however the Little Theatre was open' (*PP*, 51).

Jane Austen availed herself of the opportunities London offered for shopping. Her letters from London are full of details of small purchases, both for herself, and commissioned by others, such as muslins for gowns, and trimmings for them and for caps and bonnets, of which London offers a wider choice, as well as china at Wedgwood's shop in St James's Square. In her novels she does not pause to mention the trivia which, so absorbing in the letters, would be unnecessary frivolity. Where they do occur, they reveal both the vacuity of the person to whom they pertain, and also Jane Austen's knowledge of the London of her time. Gray's, the jewellers in Sackville Street, is the historical setting for the fictional meeting in *Sense and Sensibility* between Elinor who 'was carrying on a negociation for the exchange of a few old fashioned jewels of her mother's' (*SS*, 32) and her half-brother Mr John Dashwood. He excuses himself for not calling on her because 'one always has so much to do on first coming to town. I am come here to bespeak Fanny a seal.' Elinor has also, while waiting her turn to be served, observed a fop choosing a toothpick-case adorned with ivory, gold, and pearls. The men's characters are thus exposed by their

Covent Garden Theatre.

The interior of the Lyceum Theatre in the Strand.

occupation, the one as unbrotherly, the other as a 'puppy' (who we later find is the hero Edward Ferrars' younger brother) who has been brought thus aptly to the reader's notice.

London offers a wide variety of amusements besides shopping. Jane Austen herself gives accounts of visits to theatres, exhibitions of pictures, and concerts, while her novels mention other, even lighter amusements. She tells of visits with her nephews and nieces to the Lyceum and to Covent Garden where '*The Clandestine Marriage* was the most respectable of the performances, the rest were sing-song and trumpery, but did very well for Lizzy and Marianne [aged thirteen and twelve] who were indeed delighted; —but *I* wanted better acting'.[1] Theatrical performances were longer then than now, five or six hours altogether, and included more than one play, with opera, farce, or ballet preceding and following the main item of the evening. On a later occasion Jane Austen tells her sister of a visit to an Italian opera when 'I was very tired of Artaxerxes, highly amused with the Farce, and in an inferior way with the pantomime which followed'.[2] The type as well as the quality of what is offered varies, from *The Farmer's Wife*, which Jane Austen dismisses as 'a musical thing', to Shakespeare (she sees *Richard III* at Covent Garden and the *Merchant of Venice* at Drury Lane, with Edmund Kean, in 1814), and famous actors like the tragedian Kean, and the comedian Elliston. She goes also to concerts and to exhibitions of paintings—although no-one would guess that this was a period when much that is finest in English art had just been or was being produced. In a letter to her sister she gives a very characteristic view of the artistic scene of her time, available to the London visitor; she spends her time identifying the portraits with characters from her own novels:

> Henry and I went to the Exhibition in Spring Gardens. It is not thought a good collection, but I was very well pleased (pray tell Fanny) with a small portrait of Mrs Bingley, excessively like her. I went in hopes of seeing one of her Sister, but there was no Mrs Darcy;—perhaps however, I may find her in the Great Exhibition which we shall go to, if we have time;—I have no chance of her in the collection of Sir Joshua Reynolds' Paintings which is now showing in Pall Mall, and which we are also to visit.[3]

[1] Letter to Francis Austen, Saturday 25 September 1813.
[2] Letter to Cassandra Austen, Saturday 5 March 1814.
[3] Letter to Cassandra Austen, Monday 24 May 1813.

In her novels she mentions only amusements appropriate to personality, without local detail; in *Pride and Prejudice* Elizabeth goes with the Gardiners to the theatre but we do not hear which one; Lydia is discontent that while she is in London with them, waiting to be married, there is 'not one party, or scheme, or any thing' (*PP*, 51) even though the Little Theatre (precursor of the modern Haymarket Theatre) is open. When Harriet Smith, in *Emma*, goes to stay with the John Knightleys, to recover from her second broken heart and to visit the dentist, she is taken to Astley's Royal Amphitheatre, to see a horse-riding display something like the modern circus.

London is still small enough, and what it offers local enough, for it to be a place of chance meetings, where Colonel Brandon may hear, in a stationer's shop in Pall Mall, of Willoughby's engagement to Miss Grey, and Willoughby himself has to deliberately avoid meeting Marianne, whom he has jilted, in the course of his own and her morning expeditions in Bond Street and elsewhere.

Pall Mall.

Jane Austen does not touch upon the aristocracy, or the affairs of those who had connections with the court. Her only allusion to such is a comic one, with Sir William Lucas who, knighted when mayor of Meryton, and presented at St James's Palace, talks very improbably of meeting Mr Darcy and dancing there. The court indeed in much of Jane Austen's time was in confusion and disorder. George III had fits of madness, and had to be kept in confinement. His son, who was made Prince Regent in 1811, though popular as a young man, was later hated by many. He was supported by the Tories, while the Whigs supported his wife, the Princess of Wales; and a state of permanent rivalry existed between them. There was morally little to choose between them; both were profligate and undignified, but there was much popular feeling for the wife, whose follies were felt to be caused by her husband's, and by his neglect. Jane Austen remarked,

> Poor woman, I shall support her as long as I can, because she *is* a woman, and because I hate her husband . . . if I must give up the Princess, I am resolved at least always to think that she would have been respectable, if the Prince had behaved only tolerably by her at first.[1]

The Prince himself lived at Carlton House when in town, but spent much of his time at Brighton, with Mrs Fitzherbert, rumoured to be his legal wife. Popular distaste was expressed by Charles Lamb in a characteristically punning lampoon:

> By his bulk and by his size
> By his oily qualities
> This (or else my eyesight fails)
> This should be the Prince of Wales.

---

[1] Letter to Martha Lloyd, Tuesday 16 February 1813.

CHAPTER EIGHT

The Arts of Peace

IF one selects only the most commonly known names associated with the arts, the period of Jane Austen's adult life will include more of the most illustrious than perhaps any other period in English history. It is the period of the Romantic Revival, when for traditional taste there were still Cowper and Crabbe, recognisably eighteenth century in mode, and when the startling innovations of Wordsworth's and Coleridge's *Lyrical Ballads* (1798), Byron's *Childe Harold* (Cantos I and II, 1812), his exotic poetic tales, and Scott's early poems and ballads were changing the matter and manner of poetry. Scott's first novel, *Waverley*, appeared in 1814. In painting, the traditional modes of Sir Joshua Reynolds, and of Hogarth's satire, are giving way to the new ideas and techniques of Fuseli, Haydon, Blake, Cotman, and the early Turner. This is almost the only period of whose architects and designers the common man knows the names. He may know the earlier Wren, but here he knows the brothers Adam fully as well, while Sheraton and Hepplewhite are probably the only furniture designers known to many. The man who is familiar with any form of landscape gardening recognises Repton and 'Capability' Brown better than anyone, while those who know nothing of pottery know Wedgwood.

All the arts enjoyed a very close connection with everyday life; not only did they impinge more upon the daily round than now, but people were more conscious of the ways in which they did so, and of the aesthetic effects of commonplace and everyday matters. An easy instance is dress. The narrow high-waisted, light-fabricked, fluttering costume of women of the period, and the way they did their hair, is quite consciously based upon ancient classical models, and thus is closely linked with the general enthusiasm for the ancient world which led Lord Elgin to purchase and bring to London the marbles from the Parthenon frieze, and produced, in the architecture of the brothers Adam, all the felicities of the Greek revival.

Architecture is one of the most significant arts of any age, and is perhaps the one for which Jane Austen, in her novels, shows the most abiding concern. The people of any country that has not been crushed by war or natural destruction live with an architectural scene which is mostly that of the age before their own. The England of Jane Austen is filled with buildings dating from the Georgian period and earlier. The towns and villages were in parts even older, and it is only the wealthy, the smart, and the up-to-date who have houses, newly built, in the style we now call Regency. Architecture was very much more popularly understood than now, in that more people felt assured of sound standards of excellence, and confidence in their own judgement and taste. Gentlemen might employ architects to improve their property, but, if more modest in the scope of their alterations, depended upon their own ideas, and upon local builders, who were in turn able to work by the rules of proportion and the designs published by the great professional architects.

Along with confidence went a general appreciation and liking of what was new—as well it might, since Jane Austen's is an age which did some of its very best work in domestic building rather than in public, and on a modest as much as on a grand scale. For Jane Austen, who though she gives very few detailed accounts of houses, grounds, rooms, or furnishings shows over and over again that she is both interested and knowledgeable, 'modern' is a term of approval.

She depends upon her reader to be conversant with styles in building. She refers mainly to private houses, chiefly in the country, partly because her subjects require it, partly because they are what she knows best, but also partly because the English country house is one of the age's most original successes. Her town houses get little mention. Those in London in *Sense and Sensibility* are without detail of appearance, size, or contents: quite possibly because, giving their exact and real positions—all are in authentic London Streets like Harley Street, Hanover Square, Portman Square, or Bartlett's Buildings (Holborn)—she relies upon the reader's being familiar with their type, size, and style. But in *Persuasion* the cramped elegance of a Bath Terrace house in

Camden Place is epitomised in Elizabeth Elliot walking 'with exultation from one drawing-room to the other . . . finding extent to be proud of between two walls, perhaps thirty feet asunder' (*P*, 3).

Improving estates generally, including the building, rebuilding, and alteration of houses, is an interest very common among both nobility and gentry, to do so being both a duty and a pleasure—even becoming a passion. At the extreme are men who ruined themselves, and crippled their estates, in their lust for a greater, finer, grander house, such as George Eliot pleasantly recreates in the family of the Cheverels in *Scenes of Clerical Life*, where the new house has rooms with 'splendid ceilings and rather meagre furniture, which tells how all the spare money had been absorbed before personal comfort was thought of'.[1] A hint of such rash spending appears in *Pride and Prejudice*, at Lady Catherine's Rosings, where in the drawing-room, so Mr Collins boasts, 'the chimney-piece alone cost eight hundred pound' (*PP*, 16). This passion for building and improving manifested itself more in the country estate than the town house, in keeping with the habits of those who lived the more vital part of their lives on the land, and only visited the city. Therefore the desire for improvement naturally comprehended the grounds. Many writers who published guides as to what should be done, and how, were famous in their time, and are still well known. The most notable is probably Humphrey Repton, author of the formidably entitled *Observations on the Theory and Practice of Landscape Gardening. Including some remarks on Grecian and Gothic Architecture, collected from various manuscripts, in the possession of different noblemen and gentlemen, for whose use they were originally written; the whole tending to establish fixed principles in the Respective Arts*, published in 1803. Such works are not the prerogative only of the professional: Horace Walpole, for instance, better known as a man of letters, published a *History of Modern Taste in Gardening*.

In improvements generally, both to house and land, there are two main enthusiasms in Jane Austen's time, both of which are drawn upon in her work. The usual and accepted standards of excellence are drawn from Italy and from the classical world. The proportions on which buildings are based are those learned from

[1] 'Mr Gilfil's Love Story', Chapter 3.

classical ones, while the details and adornments are classical also. Colonnades, decorative and structural pillars, pilasters, pediments, and friezes are natural and customary in buildings of the period. The liking for such features appears inside as well as outside, in detail as well as in general, even down to the design of clocks, fire-places, and fire-irons. These classical principles had been known, used, and adapted, imaginatively and successfully, for a century and more. One of the earliest exponents is Inigo Jones, whose most famous work is probably the Queen's House at Greenwich, done as early as 1635. The best known is undoubtedly Sir Christopher Wren, whose St Paul's Cathedral was completed in 1710; and one

The West Front of St Paul's Cathedral.

of the most daring and flamboyant Sir John Vanbrugh, who finished his own contribution to Blenheim Palace in 1716.[1] In Jane Austen's own immediate era classical building had been invigorated and revived by the rediscovery—as architectural models —of Greek rather than Roman originals. Rather confusingly, they were at first termed Etruscan, because the ones first examined and admired were those from Greek settlements in Italy, not in Greece proper. The great worker in the Etruscan style is Robert Adam; Jane Austen never alludes to him, but his influence can be read almost anywhere that she alludes to building or design.

Architecture, having so much encouragement, is full of experiment. Many styles are tried besides the classical. Chinese motifs are found on furniture and china—some of it made there, though commissioned in England—Egyptian and oriental styles appear

[1] It was later completed by Nicholas Hawksmoor.

Strawberry Hill, Horace Walpole's Gothic fantasy.

in buildings like Blenheim Palace and the Brighton Pavilion. But such experiments in decoration rarely affect the proportions and principles of the structures on which they appear. The other strong influence at work at the turn of the century, does. It is the Gothic. Along with a revived interest in all things medieval in literature goes a revived interest in medieval building. One of the earliest and best known examples of Gothic revival building is Strawberry Hill, built by Horace Walpole for himself. The imitation of the medieval is of an idea, rather than of the actual; it is inaccurate and unscholarly. In early instances it is often no more than putting a few battlements, or pointed porch and windows, onto a building otherwise following classical proportions; but the idea soon burgeons and gains panache. Such panache produced William Beckford's astonishing house at Fonthill, which, intoxicated with the unclassical height of the Gothic arch, had its tower so high and narrow, on such high and narrow arches, that it collapsed.

All such experiments are plainly in the spirit of the Romantic movement as a whole, but form proof that the impulse is not scholarly or academic, when the consequences are seen in subjects which are the enthusiasms of amateurs, in the shop as well as in the salon, in wallpaper and pottery as well as churches, in women's hats as well as the major poets. Beckford is not alone as an amateur with the confidence to design what he wanted for himself. Such men, though less eccentric ones, are numerous, from the remarkable Sir John Soane, who designed the Bank of England, down to

William Beckford's house at Fonthill.

proprietors of small country cottages. The confidence undoubtedly springs from the custom of allowing young men to go on the Grand Tour to study men and manners all over the world, as an alternative or addition to studying classics at Oxford and Cambridge. The young landowner of the future saw the buildings of Italy, both the ruins of the Romans and the palaces and churches of the Renaissance, and brought back trophies and ideas. The ideas were supplemented by the books of designs and rules of connoisseurs and architects, and realised in alterations and new building when the traveller returned home and took over his patrimony. Hence the remarkably high standard not only of workmanship but also of taste, of the eighteenth and early nineteenth centuries. The common source gave uniformity, while individual confidence gave variation and originality in treatment and handling of materials.

Jane Austen herself shows this characteristic confidence, which, as a matter of course, she assumes her readers share. She bestows it upon all her characters who dabble in 'improvement' of any kind. While she discriminates between types of building, on grounds at once practical and aesthetic, many of her points depend upon the reader's familiarity with styles and conventions, and of periods besides her own. Her most obvious architectural fling is at the taste for the Gothic, of which her most obvious instance is Catherine Morland, who, her enthusiasm for all things medieval fired by her novel-reading, is sadly disappointed with Northanger Abbey:

> An abbey!—yes, it was delightful to be really in an abbey!—but she doubted, as she looked round the room, whether any thing within her observation, would have given her the consciousness. The furniture was in all the profusion and elegance of modern taste. The fire place, where she had expected the ample width and ponderous carving of former times, was contracted into a Rumford, with slabs of plain though handsome marble, and ornaments over it of the prettiest English china. The windows, to which she looked with peculiar dependence, from having heard the General talk of his preserving them in their Gothic form with reverential care, were yet less what her fancy had portrayed. To be sure, the pointed arch was preserved—the form of them was Gothic—they might be even casements—but every pane was so large, so clear, so light! To an imagination which had hoped for the smallest divisions, and the heaviest stone work, for painted glass, dirt, and cobwebs, the difference was very distressing.
>
> $\hspace{6cm}$ (*NA*, 20)

A gentler burlesque appears in *Mansfield Park,* with Fanny's lament over the chapel at Sotherton:

> Her imagination had prepared her for something grander than a mere, spacious, oblong room, fitted up for the purpose of devotion —with nothing more striking or more solemn than the profusion of mahogany, and the crimson velvet cushions appearing over the ledge of the family gallery above. 'I am disappointed,' said she, in a lower voice, to Edmund. 'This is not my idea of a chapel. There is nothing awful here, nothing melancholy, nothing grand. Here are no aisles, no arches, no inscriptions, no banners. No banners, cousin, to be "blown by the night wind of Heaven." No signs that a "Scottish monarch sleeps below." '
>
> $\hspace{6cm}$ (*MP*, 9)

The reader's appreciation of the tone of the two passages must depend upon his response to the real setting Jane Austen suggests but does not describe. General Tilney's drawing-room is in the best, most modern, taste, combining comfort with elegance. The fireplace is the proof: Rumford (1753–1814) is the inventor of the modern open fireplace with a solid, angled, fireclay surround (with which everyone is familiar), so much more efficient than the old huge chimney, with the fire standing in it in a large iron basket upon legs. Catherine should have admired. Fanny has more reason for disappointment, at seeing a chapel of James II's time, old enough only to seem old-fashioned, as the mention of crimson velvet and of mahogany—a wood popular in the age before Jane Austen's—reveals. Jane Austen, like her contemporaries, has little liking for mere age, and has therefore no intention of making Fanny ridiculous, like Catherine, for not admiring what is before her. Jane Austen does not, however, always scorn the old, though

Polesden Lacey, reputedly the original of Hartfield in *Emma*.

she likes the new. In *Emma*, Hartfield is a model of modern comfort and taste, but Donwell is equally to be esteemed:

> The house was larger than Hartfield, and totally unlike it, covering a good deal of ground, rambling and irregular, with many comfortable and one or two handsome rooms.—It was just what it ought to be, and looked what it was—and Emma felt an increasing respect for it, as the residence of a family of such true gentility, untainted in blood and understanding.
>
> (*E*, 42)

Even though what Emma thinks is not always a true guide for the reader, this is one of the times when her natural judgement is leading her right.

A man's property, and what he does with it, are almost an extension of his personality. Elizabeth Bennet, calmly approving Rosings—without Mr Collins's ridiculous raptures over the number of windows 'and what the glazing altogether had originally cost Sir Lewis de Bourgh' (*PP*, 29)—renders Lady Catherine, for a few moments, respectable; her nephew Mr Darcy becomes much more so through his own house at Pemberley, which has 'less of splendour, and more real elegance' (*PP*, 43) than Rosings. Henry Crawford, in whom Jane Austen undertakes the difficult task of delineating a sensible and attractive man who is not a virtuous one, shows sense and taste by doing well with his house and grounds at Everingham:

> 'What with the natural advantages of the ground, which pointed out even to a very young eye what little remained to be done, and my own consequent resolutions, I had not been of age three months before Everingham was all that it is now.'
>
> (*MP*, 6)

Mr Rushworth by contrast is demonstrably ineffectual for being able to do nothing with the much greater possibilities of Sotherton. The silliest improver of all is Robert Ferrars in *Sense and Sensibility*, who is an exponent of the craze for the so-called 'cottage':

> 'My friend Lord Courtland came to me the other day on purpose to ask my advice, and laid before me three different plans of Bonomi's.[1] I was to decide on the best of them. "My dear Courtland," said I, immediately throwing them all into the fire, "do not adopt either of

[1] Joseph Bonomi, A.R.A., was a fashionable architect.

them, but by all means build a cottage". And that, I fancy, will be the end of it.'

(*SS*, 35)

He goes on to instance the comforts and accommodations of a 'cottage' that contains a dining parlour, a drawing-room, a library, and a saloon. The cottage taken by the Dashwoods is an example of the modern, comfortable type:

> As a house, Barton Cottage, though small, was comfortable and compact; but as a cottage it was defective, for the building was regular, the roof was tiled, the window shutters were not painted green, nor were the walls covered with honeysuckles. A narrow passage led directly through the house into the garden behind. On each side of the entrance was a sitting room, about sixteen feet square; and beyond them were the offices and the stairs. Four bedrooms and two garrets formed the rest of the house. It had not been built many years, and was in good repair.

(*SS*, 6)

Such cottages are still to be found, and are very desirable, 'poor and small' though Jane Austen considers them when compared with a gentleman's residence. The same novel contains the most complete account of what is to be expected of the grounds of a gentleman's house:

> [Cleveland] had no park, but the pleasure grounds were tolerably extensive; and like every other place of the same degree of importance, it had its open shrubbery, and closer wood walk, a road of smooth gravel winding round a plantation, led to the front, the lawn was dotted over with timber, the house itself was under the guardianship of the fir, the mountain-ash, and the acacia, and a thick screen of them altogether, interspersed with tall Lombardy poplars, shut out the offices.

(*SS*, 41)

Cleveland has also the requisite picturesque feature in its park of 'a Grecian temple', while Longbourn in *Pride and Prejudice*, reflecting a slightly later taste, boasts 'a hermitage'.

Such features as the temple, the hermitage, and the wilderness which Longbourn also possesses are signs of the enthusiasm growing up in the latter part of the eighteenth century, alongside the classical, for the strange, the rugged, and the exotic for its own sake, in nature, art, architecture, and literature. The fashion grew rapidly for visiting places, hitherto thought wild and uncongenial, like the English Lake District (of which Elizabeth Bennet is thwarted), the Highlands of Scotland and Wales, and, in Europe, the Alps. Jane Austen, while responding to the fashion as any person of aesthetic sensibility was likely to do, has her reservations. The only place at which her own enthusiasm is expressed is in the memorable passage, already quoted, of praise of Lyme Regis. She calls upon the fashion to make her reader smile at Elizabeth Bennet's over-enthusiasm, when, offered a holiday to be spent seeing the English Lake District, she exclaims,

> 'What are men to rocks and mountains? Oh, what hours of transport we shall spend! And when we *do* return, it shall not be like other travellers, without being able to give one accurate idea of anything. We *will* recollect what we have seen. Lakes, mountains, and rivers shall not be jumbled together in our imaginations; nor, when we attempt to describe any particular scene, will we begin quarrelling about its relative situation. Let *our* first effusions be less insupportable than those of the generality of travellers.'
>
> (*PP*, 27)

But though *Pride and Prejudice* is an early novel, and *Persuasion* a late one, this is no proof that Jane Austen grew more susceptible as the movement grew, or as she grew older; for in her last work of all, the fragment called *Sanditon*, she ridicules the new habit of choosing sites for houses for their picturesque value, without regard to convenience. In *Sense and Sensibility* she allows her hero, Edward Ferrars, to burlesque the fashion;

> 'I like a fine prospect, but not on picturesque principles. I do not like twisted, crooked, blasted trees. I admire them much more if they are tall, straight and flourishing. I do not like ruined, tattered cottages. I am not fond of nettles, or thistles, or heath blossoms. I have more pleasure in a snug farm-house than a watch-tower—and a troop of tidy, happy villagers please me better than the finest banditti in the world.'
>
> (*SS*, 18)

As well as knowing the constituents of the picturesque—as Edward

'The Stamaty Family', by Dominique Ingres.

Ferrars here wittily proves his author does—Jane Austen can supply the appropriate jargon:

> 'remember I have no knowledge in the picturesque, and I shall offend you by my ignorance and want of taste if we come to particulars. I shall call hills steep, which ought to be bold; surfaces strange and uncouth, which ought to be irregular and rugged; and distant objects out of sight, which ought only to be indistinct through the soft medium of a hazy atmosphere.'

> (*ibid.*)

Along with enthusiasm for natural beauties goes enthusiasm for man-made ones. The fashion for visiting noble houses is clearly firmly established. In *Pride and Prejudice*, the Gardiners have visited several before arriving at Pemberley, Elizabeth being able to seem unwilling to go to Mr Darcy's house because 'she must own that she was tired of great houses; after going over so many, she really had no pleasure in fine carpets or satin curtains' (*PP*, 42). To guide such visitors is regularly the housekeeper's duty; Mrs Rushworth of Sotherton is humorously considered unusual in knowing her own house, having, Jane Austen ironically observes, 'been at great pains to learn all that her housekeeper could teach, and was now almost equally well qualified to show the house' (*MP*, 9).

Art, like architecture, is a topic upon which the reasonable, educated man can feel more confidence in his own judgment than anyone living in the present can do. It is closer to the useful arts than now, since portraits are the only kind of likenesses possible, and since it works closely in conjunction with interior decoration and design, pictures, both portraits and landscapes, being often an integral part of the design of rooms in great houses. Classical rediscoveries, like the Elgin marbles, purchased in 1816 and housed in the British Museum, stimulated great interest, and influenced styles of, for instance, sculptors like Nollekens and Flaxman, who classicise the costumes of their sitters, either completely, or in feeling, like Thorvaldsen's statue of Lord Byron. Even so, the classical was for using, not obeying, and alongside such sculptures is the painting of Benjamin West who, in his famous painting of the death of Wolfe (1771), broke with tradition by portraying his figures in contemporary costume. The founding of the Royal Academy by Sir Joshua Reynolds in 1768 helped to popularise painting, and the visiting of exhibitions became, as already mentioned, the habit of visitors to London.

The classic, the romantic, and the picturesque are revealed not only in the major arts, but in one of the least serious ones— costume. Although it is plain from her letters that Jane Austen takes a keen interest in dress, both a practical and a fashionable one, she is remarkably reticent in her writing about what people wear. This is prudent from a literary point of view—what is not described cannot date—and also in harmony with her principle of making detail work for her: talk about dress is a sign of frivolity. One can never deduce style from Jane Austen's remarks, only detail. This is true even in *Northanger Abbey*, which contains the most frequent allusions to costume: Henry Tilney, inventing what Catherine might write in her journal, though describing her dress, gives the reader little clue to its fashion when he says 'wore my sprigged muslin robe with blue trimmings—plain black shoes —appeared to much advantage' (*NA*, 3). If a clear picture is what is wanted, a male novelist can do better—Jane Austen's favourite, Richardson, for instance, whose description of a heroine's head-dress she herself draws on in her letters:

> A white Paris sort of cap, glittering with spangles, and encircled by a chaplet of artificial flowers, with a little white feather perking from the left ear.[1]

Jane Austen's novels cover a period in which there was a revolution in what people wore, taking place alongside the more sweeping revolutions in national affairs and the arts—as revolutions in dress so often do. Its main feature is the new use of lighter, and more perishable, materials. They arrive through the opening up of trade with the East, particularly India, which made thin cotton materials, especially muslins, cheap and easy to obtain. They are easy to wash, and therefore encourage the wearing of pale colours and of white: Edmund in *Mansfield Park* compliments Fanny on her dress by saying, 'a woman can never be too fine while she is all in white' (*MP*, 23). Such materials become common wear for the style of dress which made its appearance after the French Revolution. Women's clothes drew their inspiration from classical models—high-waisted, clinging, and flowing; men's took advantage of fine stuffs in finely-worked shirts, and elaborately-tied, high-throated cravats, which, in the hands of a master-dandy like Beau Brummel, became almost works of art.

This is an age of elegance in dress as in other things, an age when, as in other things, the urge to elegance leads to folly. Although Jane Austen does not approach the extremes which made the ladies of the French Directoire damp their gowns to give the appropriately classical folds clinging to the figure, she suggests ostentation and vulgarity through dress, as when Mrs Elton disclaims the showiness that delights her:

> 'I have the greatest dislike to the idea of being over-trimmed— quite a horror of finery. I must put on a few ornaments *now*, because it is expected of me. A bride, you know, must appear like a bride, but my natural taste is all for simplicity; a simple style of dress is so infinitely preferable to finery. But I am quite in the minority I believe; few people seem to value simplicity of dress,—and shew

---

[1] *Sir Charles Grandison*, Letter 22.

Morning and evening dresses, 1807.

and finery are every thing. I have some notion of putting such a trimming as this to my white and silver poplin.'

(E, 35)

Her comment on Emma's wedding is that it was all 'extremely shabby', with 'very little white satin, very few lace veils; a most pitiful business'. (*E*, 55). The one mine of sartorial information is Mrs Allen in *Northanger Abbey*, whose whole being is devoted to her appearance, who has one immortal conversation on the topic with the versatile and knowledgeable Henry Tilney:

'My dear Catherine,' said she, 'do take this pin out of my sleeve; I am afraid it has torn a hole already; I shall be quite sorry if it has, for this is a favourite gown, though it cost but nine shillings a yard.'

'That is exactly what I should have guessed it, madam,' said Mr Tilney, looking at the muslin.

'Do you understand muslins, sir?'

'Particularly well; I always buy my own cravats, and am allowed to be an excellent judge; and my sister has often trusted me in the choice of a gown. I bought one for her the other day, and it was pronounced to be a prodigious bargain by every lady who saw it. I gave but five shillings a yard for it, and a true Indian muslin. . . .'

'And pray, sir, what do you think of Miss Morland's gown?'

'It is very pretty, madam,' said he, gravely examining it; 'but I do not think it will wash well; I am afraid it will fray . . . but then you know, madam, muslin always turns to some account or other; Miss Morland will get enough out of it for a handkerchief, or a cap, or a cloak.—Muslin can never be said to be wasted. I have heard my sister say so forty times, when she has been extravagant in buying more than she wanted, or careless in cutting it to pieces.'

(NA, 3)

What Henry Tilney buys her is, incidentally, the material for the gown, not the made-up article.

Men's costume naturally receives less attention than women's, hence the odd little facts provided gain in importance: Henry Tilney suddenly becomes a vivid figure to the reader as well as to Catherine when 'his hat sat so well, and the innumerable capes of his great coat looked so becomingly important' (*NA*, 20). More is revealed about Bingley than the modern reader appreciates when Bennet ladies 'had the advantage of ascertaining from an upper window, that he wore a blue coat, and rode a black horse', (*PP*, 3) unless he knows that blue is a very fashionable colour for a coat at this time; later on, Lydia hopes that Wickham will be married in his blue coat, showing both that she has a frivolous mind, and that he is a fashionable scoundrel.

Children's clothes are not mentioned by Jane Austen, except for baby's caps, which the Weston's daughter, like all babies, wears—a prudent necessity in inadequately heated houses and cold bedrooms. Otherwise children are dressed as grown-ups in miniature, while boys are dressed the same as girls for the first few years. In her letters, Jane Austen refers to a nephew being 'breeched', that is, put into breeches instead of petticoats, while Coleridge, in his poem *Frost at Midnight* mentions his

> Sister more beloved
> My playmate when we both were clothed alike

The art that most closely concerns Jane Austen is, as one would expect, literature. The allusions to the works of others in her novels reveal what she herself has read, but reveal even more what she assumes her readers to have read.

Jane Austen is a novel-reader, like many women of her age and after. Her era is filled with the voices of those who protest about the quantity of novel-reading that goes on. They began before Jane Austen's time: Sheridan in *The Rivals* (1775) creates a delightful scene in which the romantic heroine Lydia Languish, expecting a visit from her aunt, hides her circulating library novels in wittily appropriate places, and puts moral works on view:

> 'Quick, quick!—Fling *Peregrine Pickle* under the toilet—throw *Roderick Random* into the closet—Put *The Innocent Adultery* into *The Whole Duty of Man*—thrust *Lord Amworth* under the sofa—cram *Ovid* behind the bolster—there—put *The Man of Feeling* into your pocket—so, so—now lay *Mrs Chapone* in sight, and leave *Fordyce's Sermons* open on the table.'
>
> (Act I, Scene 2)

in 1791 a bookseller wrote in his autobiography:

> I cannot help observing, that the sale of books has increased prodigiously within the last 20 years. According to the best estimation I am able to make, I suppose that more than four times the

number of books are sold now than were sold 20 years since. The poorer sort of farmers and even the poor country people in general, who before that period spent their winter evenings in relating stories of witches, ghosts, hobgoblins etc., now shorten the winter nights by hearing their sons and daughters read tales, romances, etc, and on entering their houses, you may see Tom Jones, Roderick Random, and other entertaining books stuck up on their bacon racks etc. If John goes to town with a load of hay, he is charged to be sure not to forget to bring home Peregrine Pickle's Adventures; and when Dolly is sent to market to sell the eggs, she is commissioned to purchase the History of Pamela Andrews. In short all ranks and conditions now READ.[1]

It is notable that by 'book' he means (as people very often do now) 'novel'. A much more violent disapprover is Coleridge:

I will run the risk of asserting, that where the reading of novels prevails as a habit, it occasions in time the entire destruction of the powers of the mind: it is such an utter loss to the reader, that it is not so much to be called pass-time as kill-time.[2]

There is no doubt that both the reading and the publishing of novels is increasing rapidly, and equally that many novels were rubbish. However, this is the beginning of the great age of the novel, which is to last all through the nineteenth century, and volume is attended with quality. Jane Austen has her own outspoken defence to the false standards that make good novels underestimated, in a famous passage from *Northanger Abbey*:

there seems almost a general wish of decrying the capacity and undervaluing the labour of the novelist, and of slighting the performances which have only genius, wit, and taste to recommend them. 'I am no novel reader—I seldom look into novels—Do not imagine that *I* often read novels—It is really very well for a novel.' Such is the common cant.—'And what are you reading, Miss—?' 'Oh, it is only a novel!' replies the young lady; while she lays down her book with affected indifference, or momentary shame.—It is only Cecelia, or Camilla, or Belinda[3],' or, in short, only some work in which the greatest powers of the mind are displayed, in which the most thorough knowledge of human nature, the happiest

[1] *Memoirs of the first forty-five years of the Life of James Lackington, Written by Himself*, 1791, as quoted in *Fiction and the Reading Public*, Q.D. Leavis, 1932.
[2] *Lectures on Shakespeare and Milton.*

[3] *Cecelia* and *Camilla* are by Fanny Burney, 1782 and 1796; *Belinda* is by Maria Edgeworth, 1801.

delineation of its varieties, the liveliest effusions of wit and humour are conveyed to the world in the best chosen language. Now, had the same young lady been engaged with a volume of the Spectator, instead of such a work, how proudly would she have produced the work, and told its name. Though the chances must be very much against her being occupied by any part of that voluminous publication, of which either the matter or manner would not disgust a young person of taste: The substance of the papers so often consisting in the statement of improbable circumstances, unnatural characters, and topics of conversation, which no longer concern any one living; and their language, too, frequently so coarse as to give no very favourable idea of the age that could endure it.   (*NA*, 5)

The passage is famous for being one of the few in the novels where Jane Austen seems to be speaking her own opinions in her own voice. Though it may not be quite so straight-faced as it sounds, it does show that the essays of Addison and of *The Spectator* are now no longer felt to be appropriate to the age, and that their function, as purveyors of instruction and morality through entertainment, is now felt to be the proper province of the novel, particularly the novel written by women (who as novelists of the period out-number men) for women to read. Jane Austen and her family were keen novel-readers, ready to defend their pursuit. In *Northanger Abbey* Jane Austen burlesques two of the popular kinds of novel— the novel of Terror, and the novel of Sensibility—while herself writing the third kind—the novel of Manners. Catherine reads, with delighted horror, Mrs Radcliffe's *Mysteries of Udolpho*, which occupies almost as much of her thoughts as does Henry Tilney, and which contains the ingredients of Gothic castles, persecuted heroines, and tyrannous villains that suggest to her that General Tilney may be a wife-murderer. It contains also the super-sensitive kind of heroine on whom Isabella Thorpe is modelling herself. The list of titles of the sensational works Isabella brings Catherine is a fine representative one: 'Castle of Wolfenbach, Clermont, Mysterious Warnings, Necromancer of the Black Forest, Midnight Bell, Orphan of the Rhine, and Horrid Mysteries' (*NA*, 6).[1] The novels Jane Austen holds up as excellent,

---

[1] Not all of these novels can now be discovered, but all are real, not invented, titles.

those by Fanny Burney and Maria Edgeworth, are, like her own, novels of manners, dealing with the contemporary, and with society, serious in morality but often humorous in tone. The great novelist of the age, beside herself, is Sir Walter Scott, who became famous almost instantaneously in 1814, with the publication of *Waverley*. Although anonymous, the book's authorship was a fairly open secret. Jane Austen herself guessed. She remarks in a humorously perverse letter to her niece Anna Austen 'Walter Scott has no business to write novels, especially good ones.—it is not fair.—He has fame and profit enough as a poet, and should not be taking the bread out of other people's mouths.—I do not like him, and do not mean to like Waverley if I can help it—but fear I must.'[1] But this is towards the end of Jane Austen's reading and writing life; in the novels she mentions Scott only for the poems, for which he was already famous by 1805, with *The Lay of the Last Minstrel*.

Poetry was much more read, and much more taken for granted as popular, even light, reading, then than now. The poet, still with the eighteenth-century sense of a coherent society, could expect to be, and was, intelligible to his contemporaries of whatever sort, sharing with them a mutual taste and mutual values. Familiarity with the best English writers is a part of every educated person's equipment, of which there are innumerable slight suggestions in the novels. How inadequate is Catherine Morland's education is suggested by her learning, at a rather late age, all the most conventional things:

> From Pope, she learnt to censure those who
>> 'bear about the mockery of woe.'
> From Gray, that
>> 'Many a flower is born to blush unseen,
>> 'And waste its sweetness on the desert air.'
> From Thompson, that
>> ... 'It is a delightful task
>> 'To teach the young idea how to shoot.'
> And from Shakespeare she gained a great store of information—
> amongst the rest that
>> ... 'Trifles light as air,

---

[1] Wednesday 28 September 1814.

> 'Are, to the jealous, confirmation strong,
> 'As proofs of Holy Writ.'
That
> 'The poor beetle, which we tread upon,
> 'In corporal sufferance feels a pang as great
> 'As when a giant dies.'
And that a young woman in love always looks
>   . . . 'like Patience on a monument
> 'Smiling at Grief.'   (*NA*, 1)

The humour of the passage is that such quotations are what everyone recognises. Shakespeare, however, is known in more than such choice gobbets; he is, as Henry Crawford remarks, 'part of an Englishman's constitution' (*MP*, 34); he is for social and family use, forming another of the entertainments for evenings at home:

> 'How many a time [says Tom Bertram] have we mourned over the dead body of Julius Caesar, and *to be'd* and *not to be'd*, in this very room.'
>   (*MP*, 13)

Henry Crawford later ingratiates himself with Fanny and the Bertrams in general by reading aloud, the rather remarkable choice of play being *Henry VIII*.

The great poets of the eighteenth century are acknowledged, very much as Browning and Tennyson are today. Catherine's education cites them; Elinor comments on Willoughby's acquaintand with them:

> 'You know what he thinks of Cowper and Scott; you are certain of his estimating their beauties as he ought, and you have received every assurance of his admiring Pope no more than is proper.'
>   (*SS*, 10)

She thus shows that Pope aroused the same mixed feelings in the Regency young woman as Tennyson in her modern counterpart. Although we are not told which contemporaries beside Cowper sent Marianne into raptures—another point at which the author leaves her reader to do his own informed guessing—in later works she tells what induces raptures in others; Fanny Price is disappointed by the Sotherton chapel, because it is not like the one in Scott's *Lay of the Last Minstrel*:

> 'There is nothing awful here, nothing melancholy, nothing grand.
> Here are no aisles, no arches, no inscriptions, no banners. No

banners, cousin, to be "blown by the night wind of Heaven". No signs that a "Scottish monarch sleeps below".' (*MP*, 9)

In *Persuasion*, another young romantic, Captain Benwick, who is in mourning for his dead fiancée, has a taste for Byron's exotic oriental tales, as well as for Scott; he discusses with Anne 'whether *Marmion* or *The Lady of the Lake* were to be preferred, and how ranked *The Giaour* and *The Bride of Abydos*; and moreover, how *The Giaour* was to be pronounced' (*P*, 11). From her letters it is easy to see Jane Austen's own enjoyment of poetry, and of another poet who only barely gets a mention in the novels: George Crabbe, significantly esteemed by that epitome of good sense and right feeling, Edmund Bertram.

The impression of contemporary taste one receives in the novels is confirmed by the various anthologies of the period; the index to one of the various editions of the *Elegant Extracts* is illuminating and delightful, comprising amongst others, Milton, Dr Johnson, John Gay (of *The Beggar's Opera*), Burns, large sections from Young's *Night Thoughts*, Goldsmith, Addison, Gray, Dryden, Cowper, Spenser, and Swift.

Serious non-fiction takes a lesser place in the novels, yet its presence can be detected. Catherine Morland, candid and uncultivated, again has her word to put in:

> 'I can read poetry and plays, and things of that sort, and do not dislike travels. But history, real solemn history, I cannot be interested in. . . . I read it a little as a duty, but it tells me nothing that does not vex or weary me. The quarrels of popes and kings, with wars and pestilences, in every page; the men all so good for nothing, and hardly any women at all—it is very tiresome: and yet I often think it odd that it should be so dull, for a great deal of it must be invention. The speeches that are put into the heroes' mouths, their thoughts and designs—the chief of all this must be invention, and invention is what delights me in other books.'
> (*NA*, 14)

Fanny Price, more intelligent and better instructed, also enjoys travel: Edmund finds Lord Macartney's *Journal of an Embassy to China* (1807) among her other books in her room. Jane Austen's own appreciation of Goldsmith's *History of England* (1764), itself a popularising of its subject, is revealed by her preposterous burlesque of it, entitled '*History of England, from the reign of Henry the*

4th to the death of Charles the 1st, by a partial, prejudiced and ignorant Historian', written before she was eighteen years old.

Jane Austen has often been charged with being irreligious, or at least with not being serious on religious matters, yet there are plenty of signs that some of her reading was very serious indeed. She is as confident in her allusions to sermons and devotional writers as to novels, and uses them in just the same ways, to make points about persons and situations. Most of these writers have sunk with as little trace as the novelists, in the present age that no longer either reads sermons, or writes them in the expectation that they will be read. Yet in the novels only the more flippant characters dislike such reading. Anne Elliot, trying to prevent Captain Benwick from indulging his melancholy with too much Byron, suggests 'the works of our best moralists, calculated to rouse and fortify the mind by the highest precepts, and the strongest examples of moral and religious endurances' (*P*, 13). Whom she means can be deduced from who is mentioned elsewhere. The first reference is a comic one. When Henry Tilney pokes fun at Catherine's use of the word 'nice', his sister explains,

> 'The word "nice" as you used it, did not suit him; and you had better change it as soon as you can, or we shall be overpowered with Johnson and Blair all the rest of the way.'   (*NA*, 14)

Dr Johnson requires no gloss; Hugh Blair, who held the chair of Rhetoric and Belles Lettres at Edinburgh University, published, as well as the Lectures to which Eleanor is referring, five volumes of sermons, to which Mary Crawford alludes when belittling Edmund's high estimate of the clergyman's office:

> 'How can two sermons a week, even supposing them to be worth hearing, supposing the preacher to have the sense to prefer Blair's to his own, do all that you speak of? govern the conduct and fashion the manners of a large congregation for the rest of the week? (*MP*, 9)

Mr Collins, asked to read aloud to the ladies

> readily assented, and a book was produced; but on beholding it (for every thing announced it to be from a circulating library), he started back, and begging pardon, protested that he never read novels . . . Other books were produced, and after some deliberation he chose Fordyce's Sermons.   (*PP*, 14)

The book is certainly Fordyce's *Sermons to Young Women*. The joke cuts two, and perhaps three, ways: Lydia, yawning and interrupting the reading, is bad-mannered, empty-headed, and frivolous; Mr Collins is a fool to expect attention to a sermon on a weekday evening, the time for amusement; while, for those who know, it is delightfully appropriate to have the polysyllabic and pompous Fordyce chosen by the wordy and windy Mr Collins.

Many of Jane Austen's best jokes spring from suppressed quotation, of the sort that comes only when the original is most thoroughly a part of both writer and reader. Such is Mrs Elton's ridiculous idiom: 'he was sure that at this rate it would be *May* before Hymen's saffron robe was put on for us' (*E*, 36). Jane Austen here uses Milton's *L'Allegro* with complete ease, and is sure that her reader is equipped to catch the allusion, and so to perceive Mrs Elton's ridiculous pretension to taste in her grotesque misapplication of it. In *Mansfield Park* Maria Bertram can suggest her captive state—prevented by a locked gate from walking in the park with Henry Crawford, and by her engagement to Mr Rushworth from associating with him—with a quotation from Sterne's *Sentimental Journey*: '"I cannot get out, as the starling said"' (*MP*, 10).

Jane Austen's juvenilia, enough of which survive to show her beginnings as a writer, reveal very plainly that literature had perhaps the greatest single influence upon her. Most of them are burlesques of popular modes, revealing by exaggeration the difference between accepted literary conventions of behaviour, motive, and sentiment, and those of real life. Like her own Anne Elliot, one could perhaps say that, beginning with 'prudence in her youth, she learned romance as she grew older' (*P*, 4). Although she happily and superbly successfully keeps within the conventional framework of the novel—the events of a young woman's life that lead to marriage—she is by no means hampered by inadequate experience or understanding of life. What she omits is often as relevant as what she stresses; her material and references reach out to most of the social concerns and developments of her day, about which they reveal, not only acquaintance, but serious thought. Jane Austen, though like Shakespeare 'not of an age, but for all time' is yet wholeheartedly, intelligently, 'rationally as well as passionately' (to use her own words), in her time.

APPENDIX I

Synopses of Novels

Northanger Abbey

Catherine Morland, aged seventeen, daughter of a clergyman and one of a family of ten, is taken on a visit to Bath by the local landowner and his wife, Mr and Mrs Allen. Here she enjoys the various entertainments of the Assembly rooms, dances, and the theatre. At one of the dances she is introduced to the young, witty, and entertaining clergyman, Henry Tilney, and in due course also to his sister Eleanor, and his father General Tilney, proprietor of Northanger Abbey. She also makes the acquaintance of Isabella Thorpe, the daughter of an old school-friend of Mrs Allen's, through whom she is introduced to the sensational Gothic novels popular at the time, particularly those of Mrs Radcliffe. The innocent and inexperienced heroine Catherine, cast by Isabella for the role of confidante, suffers various embarrassments at the hands of Isabella, an affected coquette, and her brother John Thorpe, a boaster and a liar, who arrives from Oxford with Catherine's own brother, James. John Thorpe causes her to break two social engagements with Henry Tilney and his sister and, hoping to marry her himself, he boasts of her wealth to Henry's father General Tilney. Catherine's brother, infatuated, becomes engaged to Isabella, but she is disappointed to find that the Morlands are not as rich as she thought, and flirts with the newly arrived Captain Tilney, Henry's elder brother.

General Tilney is eager to acquire Catherine and her supposed wealth in marriage for Henry, and therefore invites her to return with him and his daughter to Northanger, where Henry, though curate of the neighbouring village of Woodston, spends much of his time. Catherine is delighted to be staying both with Henry, and in a real Abbey. When she arrives, although she is disappointed by all the modern improvements the General has made, she is still in a mood to fancy mysteries—a mood intensified by imaginings with which Henry teased and entertained her on her journey. She imagines false mysteries—one when, opening an old chest in her bedroom, she finds it contains only bed-linen; the other when, late at night, she finds a mysterious roll of writing in the drawers of a black cabinet, which in the morning turns out to be a laundry list. However, she next comes upon something more like a genuine mystery, when the General not only refuses to show her one range of rooms, but forbids his daughter to do so. Catherine, discovering that the General is a man of uncertain temper, and that one of the rooms is that in which his wife died, suspects either that the General murdered her, or that he still keeps her somewhere dreadfully and mysteriously imprisoned. She determines to discover more, but when exploring the mysterious room, she is surprised by Henry Tilney, to whom she blurts out her suspicions; he gently upbraids her and brings her back to commonsense and real life.

Thereafter their association seems to advance happily, with the General taking her to visit Henry's vicarage at Woodston, as though it is to be her future home. But disaster strikes suddenly one evening when the General, who has been away, and has heard that after all Catherine has no money and no expectations, returns late at night and has her thrown out of the house first thing in the morning, to travel home by public coach as best she may. At home she is happily welcomed, but grieves silently for Henry, until he, discovering what has happened, comes after her and proposes marriage. Although they have to wait until the General, gratified when Eleanor marries a viscount (the possessor of the laundry list), gives his consent, they 'begin perfect happiness at the respective ages of twenty-six and eighteen'.

Sense and Sensibility

Elinor and Marianne Dashwood, the heroines who represent the right and wrong admixtures of sense and sensibility, are, with their mother and younger sister, rendered homeless when their father dies, and their half-brother, Mr John Dashwood, inherits the

Norland estate. John Dashwood and his wife are too cold-hearted and selfish to do much to help, in spite of the elder Mr Dashwood's dying wishes, so Mrs Dashwood takes herself and her daughters to Barton in Devon, where they rent a cottage on the estate of her kinsman Sir John Middleton. Elinor is in love with Edward Ferrars, the brother of her sister-in-law Mrs John Dashwood, but neither she nor the mother, Mrs Ferrars, approve of Elinor, who is not rich or grand enough in their eyes. Marianne, with high-flown ideas of love and romance, loses her heart to John Willoughby, a gentleman staying near Barton. Despite Elinor's warnings, Marianne has no reserves towards him, and is almost heartbroken when he suddenly leaves for London without explanation or promise to return. In the meantime she is silently loved by the middle-aged and silent Colonel Brandon. Elinor has her own, more serious troubles; although Edward Ferrars visits her, he is reserved and unhappy; and soon new visitors arrive to stay with the Middletons, two young women called Anne and Lucy Steele, both of them vulgar, prying, and self-seeking; the younger, Lucy, soon finds the opportunity to confess, secretly, to Elinor that she has been engaged to Edward Ferrars since he was a pupil of her uncle's.

Marianne's hopes and spirits revive when she and Elinor receive an invitation to go to London with Lady Middleton's cheerful, good-natured, and rather vulgar mother Mrs Jennings. When there, they meet again their step-brother and his wife, Edward Ferrars, Edward's foppish and foolish brother Robert Ferrars, their mother Mrs Ferrars, the Steele girls, and, eventually, after Marianne has written to him several times, Willoughby. But Willoughby, now paying court to a rich heiress, slights Marianne publicly, and writes her a cold and insulting note, returning all her letters. He marries the heiress and Marianne gives way to despair, for she hears in addition that Willoughby has seduced and deserted a young girl who is Colonel Brandon's ward. Meanwhile the secret of Edward's and Lucy's engagement comes out, Mrs Ferrars disowns him, and settles his income on Robert instead. However, Colonel Brandon comes to the rescue, and, through Elinor, who finds this a very painful duty, offers Edward a living and a vicarage on his estate. Edward is now able to marry Lucy, who, though not at all in love, insists on his keeping to their engagement. At this point the heroines accept an invitation to stay, on their way home to Devon, with Mrs Jennings at the home of her married daughter Mrs Palmer at Cleveland in Somerset. Marianne in her continuing misery neglects herself, gets wet, catches cold, and becomes very ill. Elinor eventually fears for her life and sends Colonel Brandon to fetch their mother. But when she thinks, late one night, that her mother has come, she runs downstairs to find that it is Willoughby. He has come in agony at Marianne's illness, to explain that he had not been trifling with her at Barton, that money and the coercion of his aunt compelled him to desert her, and that his cruel letter was written at his wife's dictation. Marianne recovers, the family returns home to Barton, Elinor hears that Lucy Steele is married. Almost immediately afterwards, to everyone's astonishment, Edward Ferrars arrives, alone and unwed, to explain that Lucy has married, not him, but his brother Robert. Elinor and he can therefore be united and live at the parsonage near Colonel Brandon, and in due course, near Marianne also, when she becomes the colonel's wife.

Pride and Prejudice

The Bennet family, comprising Mr and Mrs Bennet and their five daughters, Jane, Elizabeth, Mary, Kitty, and Lydia, live on an estate which is entailed upon their nearest male relative, the foolish clergyman Mr Collins. The daughters have no fortunes, a silly mother, some vulgar relations, and, except for Jane and Elizabeth, not much sense. Mrs Bennet's hopes are all of good marriages for them. When the young and unattached Mr Bingley rents Netherfield nearby, she marks him down for the family beauty, Jane, with what looks like a good chance of success, for the two fall in love. However, Bingley's sister Caroline and his proud and wealthy friend Mr Darcy (whom Caroline would like to marry herself) disapprove of Jane's lack of fortune and connections, persuade Mr Bingley that Jane is indifferent, and bear him away to London. Mr Darcy, however, has found himself susceptible to the lively and unconventional Elizabeth, with whom he has been thrown together when she has stayed briefly at Netherfield, to take care of Jane, who fell ill while visiting there. Elizabeth, who dislikes Darcy for finding her not handsome enough to dance with at their first meeting, suspects nothing. In the meantime a handsome stranger, Wickham, has arrived, who claims to have been deprived by Mr Darcy of a living which Darcy's father had promised him. All the girls, including Elizabeth, find Wickham fascinating. He becomes an officer in the local regiment of the militia.

The heir to the Longbourn estate, Mr Collins, pays a visit, and hopes to find a wife. He is warned off Jane by Mrs Bennet, and settles upon Elizabeth 'equally next to Jane in birth and beauty'. When he proposes and she refuses him he, in chagrin and pique, promptly proposes to Elizabeth's closest friend Charlotte Lucas who, plain and no longer young, accepts him out of a 'disinterested desire for an establishment'. They are soon married, and return to Mr Collins's parsonage at Hunsford. His patron is Lady Catherine de Bourgh, Mr Darcy's aunt, far prouder than he, and an infinitely greater snob. Elizabeth in due course pays a visit to her friend Charlotte, now Mrs Collins, and with her is invited to various social engagements at Lady Catherine's house Rosings, where she re-encounters Mr Darcy. After several meetings Mr Darcy proposes to her. Remembering how unhappy he has made Jane, and how he has, supposedly, ill-treated Wickham, she rejects him angrily and tells him why. He is surprised, hurt, and angry in his turn. Next day he gives her a letter explaining his conduct: that he did not think Jane in love with Bingley; and that Wickham has pursued an irresponsible and extravagant career, ending with an attempt to elope with Darcy's sister Georgiana, so as to get his hands on her fortune.

Elizabeth goes home confused and unhappy, to find that Jane also is not happy, having been slighted in London by Bingley's sisters and not having seen Bingley at all, and that her sisters, silly as ever, are lamenting the departure of the soldiers stationed at Meryton. Wickham has been trying to court a girl for her money, so Elizabeth is glad that she has taken the advice of her sensible aunt Mrs Gardiner, and not allowed herself to become attached to him. She begins to believe the truth of Mr Darcy's letter, and think she has misjudged him. She looks forward to her coming holiday travelling in Derbyshire and the Lakes with her aunt and uncle Gardiner. Her youngest sister Lydia then receives an invitation to accompany the militia Colonel Forster and his young wife to Brighton. Mr Bennet, despite Elizabeth's doubts, agrees. Lydia is in ecstasies. Elizabeth's own holiday is curtailed to cover Derbyshire only, and eventually takes her, unwillingly, to Mr Darcy's house at Pemberley. Here she unexpectedly meets him, and despite their mutual confusion, allows him to resume the acquaintance and introduce her and the Gardiners to his sister Georgiana. Their relationship ripens fast, but is suddenly cut off when Elizabeth receives letters from Jane to say that Lydia has run away from Brighton with Wickham—purportedly to get married at Gretna, but apparently getting no further than London. Elizabeth cannot help telling Darcy, and makes instant arrangements to return home.

Eventually the runaways are found, Wickham is bribed and persuaded, and marries Lydia quietly in London. They pay a brief visit to Longbourn on their way to Newcastle, where Wickham is to join the regular army. Lydia lets fall that Mr Darcy was present at her wedding. Elizabeth, astonished, writes to her aunt for information and learns that he has been the one who found Wickham in hiding in London, who persuaded him to marry Lydia, and who is thus the one to whom her family should be most grateful. Then Bingley unexpectedly returns to Netherfield, raising Mrs Bennet's hopes that he will after all propose to Jane, as he very soon does. Mr Darcy is with him, but relations between him and Elizabeth are uncomfortable and constrained. He leaves for a few days during which Elizabeth receives an unexpected call from Lady Catherine, who tries to make her promise not to marry Mr Darcy. Elizabeth, much surprised, refuses, and Lady Catherine, enraged, departs. Mr Darcy returns, Elizabeth thanks him for his generosity to Lydia, he proposes for the second time, and is at last made happy.

Mansfield Park

Mansfield Park is the home to which Fanny Price comes at the age of eleven, to be brought up with her wealthy cousins Tom, Edmund, Maria, and Julia Bertram, under the care of her aunt and uncle, Lady Bertram and Sir Thomas Bertram, assisted by her other, interfering aunt, Mrs Norris. She gives all her devotion to Edmund, the only one who is actively kind to her. When Fanny is nearly grown up, some new young people come to Mansfield: Mary and Henry Crawford, the half-brother and sister of Mrs Grant, wife to the rector. They soon become involved with the young Bertrams. Maria and Julia both fall in love with Henry Crawford, who flirts with both, even though Maria is engaged to the wealthy but obtuse Mr Rushworth. Mary Crawford, after trying to attract Tom, the eldest and the heir, finds herself attracted by Edmund, even though he is to become a clergyman. Early acquaintance, and the conduct of all when a day's visit is paid to Mr Rushworth's home at Sotherton, make Fanny understand that the Crawfords, though charming, are unscrupulous and lacking in principle, and that Edmund is in love with Mary, though not recklessly enough to give up his chosen profession to please her. Sir Thomas Bertram has to leave the country to attend to his West Indian estates; in his absence, the young people, freed from his authority and good sense, and fired by the enthusiasm of Tom's friend Mr Yates, prepare to put on a performance of a mawkish and sentimental play. Fanny and Edmund alone disapprove. Everyone behaves badly: the flirtation between Henry Crawford and Maria intensifies, Mr Rushworth becomes jealous, Julia sulks, and eventually even Edmund is persuaded to act, to relieve Mary from embarrassment. Sir Thomas arrives just in time to stop the performance. Crawford leaves without giving Maria any hope that he will marry her, so, in rage and despair, she marries Mr Rushworth. Julia accompanies her on her wedding tour.

Fanny becomes more valued when her cousins have gone, both at home and as a friend for Crawford. Henry Crawford, meeting her again at dinner at the parsonage, is attracted, and decides 'to make Fanny Price in love with [him]'. He very soon renders *himself* in love with *her*. He is enabled to earn her gratitude by arranging that her sailor brother William, who pays a visit to Mansfield, shall be promoted to a lieutenancy, but on the other hand distresses her by tricking her into accepting the gift of a gold necklace, which she had suppose to be from Mary. After a ball, given by Sir Thomas to celebrate William's visit and Fanny's entry into society, William returns to Portsmouth, where the Price family live, Crawford goes to London, and Edmund goes to Cambridge to be ordained, much to Mary's distress, since she is still determined not to marry a clergyman. Henry Crawford returns, proposes to Fanny, and is refused. Everyone is shocked at her for rejecting so good a match, and Fanny is very miserable; even Edmund hopes she will come in time to love Henry, being now blind to both his faults and Mary's.

Sir Thomas, thinking that Fanny is too complacent about her comforts at Mansfield to appreciate the chance of marriage, proposes that she should go home to her parents on a visit. She is glad to do so. However, the family house at Portsmouth is a sad shock: her father is lazy, her mother a disorganised slattern, the house small, badly-run, and full of disorderly children. Fanny manages to make friends with her younger sister Susan, who is eager to learn from her.

The disasters of the climax begin when, as Fanny learns in letters, Tom Bertram falls so seriously ill that his life is in danger. Henry Crawford visits Portsmouth and calls on Fanny, making a good impression on her by his own behaviour, and by the contrast he presents to her uncomfortable surroundings. Fanny keeps up a correspondence with Mary Crawford in London (who now views Edmund as the prospective heir of Mansfield) and expects continually to hear that Edmund has proposed to her, and been accepted. The storm actually breaks when, after an anxious letter from Mary denying rumours not stated, it becomes public that Maria, now Mrs Rushworth, has left her husband and eloped with Henry. Julia, fearing her father may be very strict with her since Maria's disgrace, makes a runaway marriage with Mr Yates. The misery of the Mansfield family is complete when Edmund hears Mary's frivolous and irresponsible comments on, not the sin, but 'the folly of our two relations'. He comes and takes Fanny and Susan back to Mansfield to comfort Lady Bertram. Maria, divorced by her husband, eventually realises that Henry will never marry her and leaves him. She and Mrs Norris, whose favourite she has always been, and whose influence on her has all been bad, live together in seclusion. Tom recovers, and Edmund at last becomes 'as anxious to marry Fanny, as Fanny herself could desire'.

Emma

Emma Woodhouse 'handsome, clever, and rich' lives happily with her semi-invalid father at Hartfield, in the village of Highbury. When the novel opens, her close friend and former governess has just married Mr Weston, leaving Emma lonely, but complacently congratulating herself that she has encouraged and brought about the match. She has still, however, the company of Mr Knightley, the owner of the neighbouring Donwell estate, whose younger brother John Knightley is married to Emma's elder sister Isabella. She soon finds a new friend in Harriet Smith, a pretty young girl, 'the natural daughter of somebody', who boards with the local schoolmistress Mrs Goddard. Emma is soon seized with the idea that Harriet should marry the personable local vicar, Mr Elton. Although Harriet herself is half in love with a local farmer, Robert Martin, Emma encourages her to look higher, and think herself worth a better man. Mr Knightley disagrees, but Emma will not listen. She encourages Mr Elton to visit them, particularly while she is drawing Harriet's portrait, which he effusively admires. Mr Elton misinterprets Emma's encouragement and aspires to marry her, while she assigns his compliments to Harriet, not herself. After a Christmas party at the Weston's he proposes to Emma, disastrously, and is refused. Emma is ashamed of herself, very sorry for Harriet, and resolute to reform.

Her resolution is soon put to the test. Two newcomers arrive. One is Jane Fairfax, the beautiful and talented young niece of Miss Bates, who comes to stay with her aunt and grandmother to recover her health before beginning a career as a governess. She has been brought up as companion to a girl her own age who has just married a Mr Dixon. The second newcomer is Mr Weston's son by his first wife: Frank Churchill is an attractive young man who has been brought up by his aunt and uncle and now bears their name. Emma's fancy now takes two flights: one that she may be in love with Frank and he with her, the other that Jane Fairfax has had an unhappy love affair with her friend's husband Mr Dixon. As Frank Churchill knows both Jane and the Dixons, she admits her suspicions to him. He encourages her in them, especially when Jane receives the gift of a piano, from an unknown giver. Mrs Weston wonders whether Mr Knightley is in love with Jane: Emma is indignant, and Mr Knightley, when it is hinted, denies it.

Mr Elton, meantime, has removed himself from danger and recovered his self-esteem by marrying a young woman of fortune but no breeding. She queens it over Highbury, patronises Emma, and enthusiastically 'takes up' Jane Fairfax. When the Westons arrange a long-promised ball at the Crown Inn, Mrs Elton takes it as a compliment to herself. Mr Elton shows his pique at Emma by refusing to dance with her friend Harriet. Mr Knightley shows himself a true gentleman by asking her himself.

The following day, Harriet, out walking, is molested and threatened by some gipseys but rescued by Frank Churchill. On a later occasion, she confesses to Emma that, quite recovered now from her devotion to Mr Elton, she thinks someone else superior. Emma assumes this must be Frank, begins mental match-making again, and gives guarded encouragement. Meanwhile Mr Knightley begins to suspect an association between Frank and Jane.

Tensions in Highbury begin to build up. At a picnic at Donwell Jane is heard refusing to accept a governess-ship with a friend of Mrs Elton's, and soon goes home distressed and weary. Frank arrives immediately afterwards unaccountably angry. The following day, on an outing to Box-hill, Frank flirts wildly with Emma, Jane seems ill, and Emma is unforgivably rude to Miss Bates. Mr Knightley rebukes her, and she goes home in tears. The following day her repentance makes her call on Miss Bates, where Jane who is now really ill, refuses to see her. She learns that Frank Churchill has left to return to his uncle and ailing aunt at Richmond, and that Jane has suddenly accepted the post with Mrs Elton's friend. Mr Knightley goes away to stay with his brother in London.

The resolution of all the novel's mysteries and misunderstandings begins when Frank's aunt Mrs Churchill suddenly dies. Everyone then discovers that Frank has been secretly engaged all the time to Jane Fairfax, but concealing the truth because his aunt would have disapproved. Emma is astounded, and thinks Harriet will be in despair, but is astounded again to find that Harriet has fixed her heart, not on Frank, but on Mr Knightley himself. 'It darted through [Emma], with the speed of an arrow, that Mr Knightley must marry nobody but herself.' Emma's unhappiness remains uneased until Mr Knightley himself returns, hoping to comfort Emma for what he thinks she must be suffering from finding out that Frank is engaged to Jane. His attempt at consolation soon turns into a proposal of marriage. Harriet is sent on a visit to London, to comfort her in her third disappointment, which, however, lasts only till she again meets there her first admirer Robert Martin whom, now Emma's influence is removed, she happily accepts. Everyone is happy, even Mr Woodhouse, who is brought to agree to Emma's marriage by two circumstances: one that Mr Knightley nobly offers to live at Hartfield so that Emma can continue to look after her father; the other that the hen-roost is robbed, so that Mr Woodhouse feels glad to have a man in the house.

Persuasion

Eight years before the novel begins, Anne Elliot has been persuaded by her family and her friend, Lady Russell, to break off her engagement to a young sailor, Captain Wentworth, because he has no money and his prospects are too uncertain. When the novel opens, her father, Sir Walter Elliot, and her elder sister, Elizabeth (with whom Anne, unmarried and unchanged, still lives at Kellynch Hall), have discovered that they have so much overspent their income that they will have to let Kellynch and move to Bath. By a coincidence the new tenants are to be Admiral and Mrs Croft, the sister and brother-in-law of Captain Wentworth.

When the Elliots leave, Elizabeth would rather have the company of her young widow friend Mrs Clay than her sister, so

Anne goes on a visit to her younger married sister, Mary Musgrove, who lives at Uppercross with her husband, Charles (who once proposed to Anne) and her two small sons. Here Anne is thrown into the society of Charles's parents, and his two young and lively sisters Henrietta and Louisa. The Crofts soon make their acquaintance, and are soon visited by Captain Wentworth. Anne finds that he no longer wishes to know her, and that both Henrietta and Louisa find him fascinating. However, he admires Louisa most, for having the more determination (contrasting her with Anne, who gave way to her friend's persuasion). Henrietta soon returns to her former admirer, her cousin Charles Hayter. Louisa seems almost engaged to Captain Wentworth.

A visit of pleasure is arranged to Lyme Regis, to which all the young people go, where they meet Wentworth's naval friends the Harvilles, and Captain Benwick, who is in mourning for his fiancée, Harville's sister. Benwick finds Anne sympathetic and attractive. A stranger staying at the same inn also admires her. On an early morning walk along the shore, Louisa shows her determination by insisting on jumping down some stone steps, slips, bumps her head, and gets severe concussion. The only one of the party to keep presence of mind is Anne. Captain Wentworth feels responsible for Louisa's accident, several times appeals to Anne for advice, and wants her to stay and nurse Louisa; but Anne's sister Mary, feeling left out, insists on staying herself.

Anne returns to her friend Lady Russell, and accompanies her to Bath, where they find the Elliots enjoying their new acquaintance, who include a cousin, Mr William Elliot, heir to the Kellynch estate. He is the stranger who admired Anne at Lyme. Mrs Clay meanwhile is plainly trying to attract Sir Walter.

In Bath, Anne also meets a friend, a Mrs Smith, who had befriended her at school; she is now poor, widowed, bedridden, and crippled with rheumatism. She has formerly known Mr Elliot, who was a friend of her husband's. The Crofts come to Bath for the Admiral's health, bringing a letter from Mary, by which Anne learns to her great surprise that Louisa, though still not completely recovered, has become engaged to Captain Benwick. Wentworth is now free, and proves it by coming to Bath. But he is discouraged in seeking a new acquaintance with Anne by seeing the attentions of Mr Elliot, whom Lady Russell favours as a husband for Anne, though Anne not only does not love him but does not fully trust him.

   Anne finally learns from Mrs Smith that Mr Elliot, though now eager to be respectable and respected as a future baronet, has lived a dissolute life, has partly caused Mrs Smith's husband's poverty, and, though appointed executor of his will, has refused to act; he is therefore greatly responsible for Mrs Smith's plight. Anne is shocked, but, before she is able to reveal what she knows, calls on the Musgroves, who have arrived in Bath to buy wedding-clothes for the two daughters. Here she is engaged in a conversation on fidelity with Captain Harville, in which she claims for women the power 'of loving longest, when existence or when hope is gone'. Captain Wentworth overhears her enough to make him write a letter renewing his proposals of marriage of eight years before. Anne, so much upset that she seems ill, is escorted part of the way home by her brother-in-law, but they meet Captain Wentworth, who is happy to change places. Nothing can now prevent their marrying and being happy. Mrs Smith's finances are put straight, Mr William Elliot gives up his hopes of marrying into the baronet's family, and Mrs Clay gives up her hopes of marrying the baronet Sir Walter, for the hope of marrying the future baronet Sir William.

APPENDIX 2

Biography of Jane Austen

Jane Austen's life was neither long nor eventful. She was born at Steventon, a small village in Hampshire, near Basingstoke, on 16 December 1775, and lived only forty-two years. She was the youngest of the seven children of the rector George Austen, and his wife Cassandra (née Leigh). The only claim to literary distinction in her ancestry is that Mrs Austen's uncle was Dr Theophilus Leigh, a master of Balliol College, Oxford, and a noted wit.

Jane Austen lived at Steventon until she was twenty-six, with the exception of one short period when she went to school at Reading; she was at the time too young for it to do her much good, but went to be with her sister Cassandra, three years older than herself, from whom she was inseparable, and who was all her life the person closest to her in a family of close affections. Jane Austen had no formal education, but her claim to be 'unlettered' is comic hyperbole. She was instructed both by her father and by her eldest brother James (more than ten years older than herself) who was a clergyman like his father, and became rector of Steventon after him. Her second brother, Edward, was adopted by some cousins named Knight, and inherited their estates at Godmersham in Kent. He is the father of a large family of which the eldest, Fanny, was favourite niece of Jane Austen's, to whom she wrote some of her most revealing letters. The third brother, Henry, who super-intended the publication of her novels, had an uncertain career, once went bankrupt, and eventually became a clergyman. He lived in London, with a wife who was the widow of a French aristocrat guillotined in the Revolution; Jane Austen stayed with them on visits to London. The two youngest brothers, Francis and Charles, both joined the navy, both saw active service, and both eventually became admirals. It is on them that Jane Austen draws in her novels where sailors and the navy appear, even using the names of ships to which they belonged.

Neither Jane Austen nor Cassandra married, but lived all their lives with their mother. Cassandra was once engaged to a young army chaplain, who unfortunately died in the West Indies. There are rumours that Jane Austen also was engaged to a young man who died, but the resemblance of the hints to her sister's known circumstances is rather too close to lcok like truth. She certainly received at least one proposal that she refused.

As a writer, Jane Austen began young, with private, comic burlesques of literary modes, written for family entertainment only. It is not easy to date the earliest of her novels—*Northanger Abbey, Sense and Sensibility,* and *Pride and Prejudice*—since they existed in some form when she was in her early twenties, but were not published until much later. All of them were much revised by their painstaking author, as is proved by the fact that *Sense and Sensibility,* at least, originally existed as a novel in letters.

In 1801 Mr Austen retired, and moved with his wife and daughters to Bath, where they lived until her father died in 1805, when they moved, in rather straitened circumstances, to lodgings in Southampton, a place convenient for keeping in touch with the sailor brothers and their families. In 1809 they made their final move, to Chawton, near Alton, to a cottage given to them by their brother Edward Knight. Jane Austen lived there until just before her death, on July 18 1817, at Winchester, where she had gone to be near to expert medical care. Her life was spent without great events, but diversified by long visits to relations, particularly to her brother Edward at Godmersham, after he was left a widower with a family of twelve children.

Her novels were all published during the last period of her life, at Chawton: *Sense and Sensibility* first, in 1811, then *Pride and Prejudice,* 1813, *Mansfield Park,* 1814, *Emma,* 1816, and *Persuasion* and *Northanger Abbey* posthumously in 1818. The odd one is *Northanger Abbey,* which was one of the first to be written, though published last. It was probably written in 1798, was prepared for the press in 1803 and sold to a publisher in Bath (for £10), who did not print it; after her first two novels had appeared Jane Austen managed to buy back the manuscript for the original sum, but did nothing further with it, possibly because it is so much shorter than the customary length for a three-volume novel, and would also be, by this time, somewhat out of date in its picture of Bath life.

Jane Austen made little money from her novels, and did not have a large public. She was, however, admired by men as distinguished as Sir Walter Scott, had her last books brought out by John Murray, the friend and publisher of Lord Byron, and dedicated *Emma*, at his own request, to the Prince Regent.

Index

References to Jane Austen herself, the titles of her novels, and the characters in them occur so frequently that page-references to them would be too extensive to be useful. They therefore do not figure in the index, which comprises people other than Jane Austen, titles of works by other authors, place-names, and topics discussed in the text.